D0125763

Contents

Prologue

IT WAS 1913. THE THREE-YEAR *sea expedition had started off badly and was rapidly getting worse. Personal and professional conflicts were straining relations among scientists and crew on board the* Karluk *as they cruised toward the Western Arctic. Now their ship was in peril, held fast in the frozen embrace of an ice pack in the Beaufort Sea and drifting helplessly away from shore. The amazing power of the ice was crushing the life from their vessel, and they could do nothing to stop it.*

The scientists had sought a close-up encounter with the Arctic, and they were getting it: ice was the enemy, and it was winning. Sub-zero temperatures caused loose ice around the Karluk *to build into a solid mass and fuse to the hull. The immense pressures threatened to destroy the party's only transportation and shelter. Multi-year sea ice, up to thirty metres thick, was a major hazard to wooden-hulled ships, even if they were reinforced for northern waters. There was no room to manoeuvre or push the vessels through to open water—not that any open water could be seen. The winter darkness, low clouds, and fog restricted visibility to the few metres of glacial ridges thrusting up all around them. Wind-driven moisture caused more ice, a thick coat of it, to build up on one side of the ship. The rigging made the structure top-heavy, resulting in a steep list to the side. Walking below deck was dangerous. Supplies had shifted out of their storage bins, and the disoriented men stumbled through tilted doorways and along angled floorboards.*

Things were even worse outside. When the men went to fish or hunt seal to supplement their diet, they discovered just how inadequate their clothing was. The wind drove snow and sleet horizontally that cut into their faces and made them bleed—and froze them to the bone. Some tried sewing two parkas together, but they still could not keep warm. Their hands were so stiff with cold, they were hardly able to cast fishing line off the spools or harness the dogs to a sled.

Sledding was difficult too, even though the dogs spread out in a fan formation to travel over the ice. The driver, or musher, often had to jump off the sled runners and push to help the dogs pull the sled over uplifted masses of jagged ice; he would then have to try slowing the almost-vertical descent down the other side. Often, the dogs had to be fitted with protective leather booties to keep their paws from getting scraped and prevent ice balls from forming on their footpads. Such irritations could cause dogs to go lame.

The men dared not venture too far. To be stranded on the ice, not knowing the way back to the ship, would be a death sentence. This was hostile territory, and they were unprepared for the life-or-death challenges they faced. The scientists, and much of the crew, had limited experience living off the land, let alone surviving the hardships of the North. They were out of their element, and they knew it.

CHAPTER

1

The Grand Adventure

IT WAS TO BE A grand adventure, charting new land masses for the young country of Canada in the Western Arctic and conducting scientific research. While the major countries in Europe were gearing up for what would become the First World War (1914–1918), which would soon involve Canada, scholars in North America were pursuing a different course. The Canadian Arctic Expedition (CAE) was the first multidisciplinary scientific expedition to explore north of Alaska and the Beaufort Sea. It was as exciting as space travel is today. The brainchild of Manitoba-born American explorer/anthropologist Vilhjalmur Stefansson, this endeavour would build upon his northern work after the Stefansson–Anderson Expedition of 1908–1912 ended. That expedition had conducted an anthropological and zoological survey of the central Arctic coast for the American Museum of Natural History and had been marked by clashes between Dr. R.M. Anderson, an academic and polar zoologist who worked strictly according to scientific principles, and Stefansson, who marched to his own drummer. The personality conflicts during that undertaking would be echoed in greater discord on this expedition and lead to terrible misfortune.

Stephansson was born William Stephenson (*not* the "Man Called Intrepid"!) in 1879 at Gimli, Manitoba, to parents who had emigrated from Iceland two years earlier. The family moved to North Dakota in 1880 after devastating floods caused the deaths of two other children. During his university years, William changed his name to Vilhjalmur Stefansson. In 1904 and 1905, he studied the language and dietary habits of Icelanders. In 1906, he joined the Leffingwell–Mikkelsen Arctic expedition as its ethnologist but failed to meet up with other expedition members at the Mackenzie River delta: he had unilaterally decided to spend the winter living among the Inuit. From 1908 to 1912, Stefansson led an expedition back to the Arctic, exploring northern Alaska east to the Canadian Arctic Archipelago.

Stefansson initially approached US sponsors to fund the Canadian expedition but collected only $45,000, which would finance one ship and a crew of six. He needed more money, and so he looked north. Seeking to establish Canadian sovereignty over potential new land discoveries, and fearing what would happen if an American-backed consortium found new land in his own backyard, Prime Minister Sir Robert Borden agreed to fund the entire expedition. Two government agencies were assigned management responsibility for the expedition: the Geological Survey of Canada, and the Department of Naval Service, under the Hon. J.D. Hazen, who was also the Minister of Marine and Fisheries. Dr. Reginald W. Brock, Director of the Geological Survey, insisted on research studies being conducted along the Canadian Arctic mainland coast. The North American Arctic was, he said, "the last remaining place in the world where great geographical discovery was possible."

In an early statement, Stefansson stated he would only be hiring British subjects, but the CAE would be a three-year multidisciplinary, multinational enterprise, employing fourteen scientists from Australia, Portugal, Norway, Holland, and Scotland, as well as Canada and the US, plus the ships, captains, and crews to transport them. Initial costs were estimated at $75,000. Since the official objectives were now twofold, the expedition was administratively subdivided: the water-based Northern Party, led by Stefansson, would search for new lands north of the mainland. The land-based Southern Party, led by Dr. R.M. Anderson, would conduct scientific documentation of flora, fauna, geology, geography, resources, and archaeology on the northern mainland, from Alaska east to Coronation Gulf. The Northern Party, in addition to looking for land, was to undertake a program of through-the-ice depth soundings to map the edge of the continental shelf, along with conducting meteorological, magnetic, and marine biological studies.

Stefansson decided (again, unilaterally) to assume command over both parties and insisted he be the sole contact for media inquiries and publication. He also left the multitude of CAE administrative details to Dr. Anderson, thus freeing himself to focus on his preferred activity—self-promotion.

At this time, the existence of large, undiscovered land masses, in addition to the Arctic Archipelago, or even a small continent in the semi-enclosed Arctic Ocean, north of the Beaufort Sea above Alaska and Siberia, was considered possible. One proponent of this theory was Dr. R.A. Harris of the US Coast and Geodetic Survey. Nobody knew for sure because nobody had thoroughly explored the area. But Stefansson believed it was there, under the polar ice cap, and he intended to find it.

According to Stefansson,

> The main work of the party aboard their ship was to be the exploration of the region lying west of the Parry Islands and especially that portion lying west and northwest from Prince Patrick Island. She was to sail north approximately along the 141st meridian until her progress was interfered with either by ice or by the discovery of land. If land were discovered a base was to be established upon it, but if the obstruction

> turned out to be ice an effort was to be made to follow the edge eastward with the view of making a base for the first year's work near the southwest corner of Prince Patrick Island, or, failing that, on the west coast of Banks Island.

For those who could follow such directions, all would be well. The main expedition ship was to head directly to Herschel Island, but if she encountered ice and was forced to drift, then theories about the direction of Arctic currents could be tested. Would they, perchance, drift across the North Pole all the way to the shores of Greenland? Their scientific dredging of sea-floor sediments and depth soundings could unearth new mineral deposits and create more accurate nautical charts. A million square miles in the Arctic was still marked on maps as "unexplored territory." The possibilities were endless. It was a scientist's dream assignment.

* * *

The official direction issued by the federal government was science first, but not at the expense of safety: "The Chief of the Expedition will be careful not to endanger the lives of the party, and while neglecting no opportunity of furthering the aim of the Government, he will bear in mind the necessity of always providing for the safe return of the party. The safety of the ship itself is not so important." But this was not Stefansson's philosophy. While Stefansson accepted co-leadership of the expedition, his intent was to operate as a free agent, accepting federal funding but not being constrained by federal directives.

He promoted a grandiose vision of the North as a populous region capable of supporting many more inhabitants and ripe for commercial development. He saw the Northwest Passage as a strategic "polar Mediterranean," controlled by Canada, as an economic powerhouse of the twentieth century. He schemed to develop a large-scale meat-and-wool industry by domesticating muskoxen, importing Norwegian reindeer, and then integrating native caribou into vast herds. His plan fell through because he did not consider how all those animals could be fed.

His selection of a ship for the first Canadian Arctic Expedition was equally flawed.

CHAPTER

2

Flagship of the Northern Party

THE *KARLUK*, A WHALER OF 321 gross tonnage, 39 metres long and 7 metres wide, powered by sail and a 150-horsepower auxiliary coal-fired steam engine, was the expedition's sole supply ship and, by default, its flagship. Like most ships of her type, she was made of wood and did not have a wireless radio for communications, although she was equipped with an emergency medical kit.

She had been built in 1884 at Benicia, California, for the Alaska salmon trade (*karluk* is the Aleut word for fish) and rigged as a brigantine, with two masts, the foremast equipped with square sails. In 1892, she was bought for use on the new whaling grounds near Herschel Island, and her bow and sides were reinforced with five-centimetre

Australian ironwood. She completed fourteen whaling voyages, overwintering five times in the North. She sat idle in San Francisco from 1911 to 1913, when Theodore (C.T.) Pedersen, a Norwegian captain, fur trader, and long-time friend of Stefansson who had been offered the position of skipper, suggested her for the expedition. He claimed that of four ships available, the *Karluk* was "the soundest and best adapted for our purpose." Stefansson bought her at the bargain price of $10,000, which he charged back at cost to the Canadian government, his new financial backer. Pedersen sailed her up the coast to Victoria, BC, to set off from there as lead ship of the CAE's Northern Party.

Several designations were applied to the *Karluk*, including "HMCS" (His Majesty's Canadian Ship), "DGS" (Dominion Government Ship), and "CGS" (Canadian Government Ship). HMCS was used for Royal Canadian Navy (RCN) ships, and the *Karluk* flew the Canadian Blue Ensign of the RCN, although she sailed under a non-navy captain and with a non-navy crew. The ship spent most of April and May 1913 undergoing repairs and refitting at the naval dockyard in Esquimalt, BC. The dry dock at Esquimalt, a key repair facility and a long-time naval base for the British army, was just what was needed to get the *Karluk* shipshape.

While work was under way, Pedersen happened to read a newspaper account of a speech given by Stefansson in New York in which he was quoted as saying that if the *Karluk* could not reach the intended destination of Herschel Island, then

The Canadian Arctic Expedition flagship, HMCS *Karluk*, at Esquimalt, BC, on June 17, 1913. LIBRARY AND ARCHIVES CANADA C-032638T

he would have her steam north as far as possible and freeze her into the ice pack as a base from which to look for new land. Pedersen was enraged. As an experienced northern mariner, he knew that strategy was dangerous. Freezing that far into the ice was not survivable without steel plating and beam reinforcement. But, aware that Stefansson would probably demote him and appoint an inexperienced navigator over him if he objected to the plan, Pedersen abruptly resigned and returned to San Francisco to captain the schooner *Elvira*, which was involved in whaling and trading in the North Pacific and Arctic Oceans. Since the expedition was to depart in June, that left a big vacancy at the top of its transportation hierarchy.

The position was offered to thirty-six-year-old Robert Abram "Bob" Bartlett, the burly, blaspheming son of a seafaring family from Brigus, Newfoundland. On the culture side, he loved music and was fond of reading classical works by Shakespeare and Homer's *Odyssey*. He was, as the saying goes, "between assignments," hoping to join an expedition to Antarctica but in the meantime working with the spring seal hunt off the coast of Newfoundland. His last great adventure had been the expedition to find the North Pole with American explorer Admiral Robert E. Peary in 1909, and Bartlett was restless to begin another polar voyage, north or south. He missed the ocean, the wind, the ice, the life on board ship. He only felt at home when he was out at sea, so when the telegram came from Stefansson, he accepted, in spite of misgivings about the type of ship he would captain.

Bob Bartlett's mother had sent him to a Methodist college in hopes he would become a minister, but to no avail. He chose to spend six years completing his Master Certificate at Halifax's Nautical Academy so he could captain a ship. Bartlett's polar exploration career began in 1898 when he was asked to serve as first mate aboard the *Windward*, flagship of Admiral Peary's North Pole Expedition. (The *Windward* became frozen in sea ice near Ellesmere Island, and Peary was unable to complete the trek to the Pole overland by sledge.)

Between 1898 and 1909, Captain Bartlett and Admiral

Peary made three separate attempts to reach the North Pole. After the 1898 voyage, Bartlett next captained Peary's ship the SS *Roosevelt* on the Arctic expedition of 1905–06, this time reaching the northern tip of Ellesmere Island. The *Roosevelt* had been especially designed to get as far north as possible through polar ice. It had egg-shaped sides, allowing it to ride high on ice; a strong but flexible seventy-six-centimetre-thick hull; large crossbeams; a flared, narrow prow to cut through ice; and a powerful engine. In spite of the ship's features, the expedition was abandoned because, in July 1906, sea ice had pummelled the boat, crushing its rudder and breaking two propellers. Bartlett managed to get the *Roosevelt* to Greenland to be repaired, but it was damaged again in September on its way south. On Christmas Eve of 1906, Bartlett steered the *Roosevelt* into New York's harbour. "The poor old *Roosevelt*, as well as ourselves, was ready for the insane asylum or the dump heap," he wrote in his logbook.

In 1908, Peary made a third attempt (on the repaired *Roosevelt*) to reach the Pole, and Bartlett accompanied him again, but only to the final stage of Peary's land trek. By the end of March, the expedition members were within 241 kilometres of the Pole. At this point, Peary gave Bartlett orders to head back to Ellesmere Island and instead brought along Peary's friend, Matthew Henson. Bartlett was heartbroken. "It was a bitter disappointment," Bartlett later told the *New York Herald*. "I don't know, perhaps I cried a little."

Peary's contention that he was the first white man to

have travelled overland to the geographic North Pole was immediately challenged. Reporters with American newspapers covering the quest agreed he had crossed miles of Arctic desert and approached his target but had not gone all the way. Without trained navigators capable of making the required technical calculations, Peary's achievement was suspect.

Denied a polar achievement, Bartlett made the best of a bad situation on that final trip with Peary by deciding to at least reach the 88th parallel north before returning south. Leaving camp, he walked a solitary route north for about eight kilometres and retraced his steps back. But his readings showed he had only reached latitude 87°47' north. Fierce winds had shifted the ice floes south, and Bartlett missed his mark. He had already travelled farther north when he had recorded latitude 87°48' in late March, but it still beat the previous farthest-north record reached by Peary in 1906. Bartlett received public accolades, and the American National Geographic Society's prestigious Hubbard Medal for Arctic exploration, for reaching and recording latitude 87°48' north in the spring of 1909—at 209 kilometres from the Pole, the farthest recorded distance north any human being had travelled.

Bartlett gallantly defended Peary against critics who doubted Peary's claim to have reached the Pole. He stated in his logbook, "I must chuckle again when I think of people saying that Peary didn't go to the Pole. It was an easy jaunt to the Pole from where I left him, and conditions were improving right along."

Bartlett agreed to captain a ship for a fourth polar expedition, this one funded by millionaire sportsmen Harry Whitney and Paul Rainey in 1910. It was solely a shooting expedition, not a scientific or research mission. On their return, whatever else they may have shot, the American hunters presented the Bronx Zoo with two live polar bears.

Although Bartlett never reached the North Pole or transited the Northwest Passage, his northern trips sparked a lifelong obsession with Arctic exploration at the top of the world. He was just what Stefansson needed now on the *Karluk*.

CHAPTER

3

The Team Assembles

PEARY HAD RECOMMENDED BARTLETT TO Stefansson when the latter was searching for a replacement skipper. Bartlett was Stefansson's second choice, and he knew it. When Bartlett arrived at Esquimalt in early June, the *Karluk* had undergone extensive overhauling, but when Bartlett inspected his expedition ship, he immediately ordered additional repairs and upgrades including a new stern-post, new water tanks, new sails, and a complete overhaul of the engine, to the tune of $4,000. All this would maybe bring her up to what he considered minimum standard. Her decks were dirty, piled high with drums of oil, sacks of coal, crates of supplies, ropes, tools, and large skin boats called umiaks. Underneath all this, he could see that the wooden planking was stained and weather-beaten. The decks creaked as he walked across them. Below deck was no better. The cabins were unpainted and had not been decluttered from the detritus of previous occupants. The boat reeked of whale oil. Her engine was, in the words of chief engineer John Munro, "an old coffee pot."

Although built to be a sturdy whaler, the *Karluk*, unlike the *Roosevelt*, had not been built to withstand ice pressure; few ships of the time were. When he inspected the quickly assembled crew, Bartlett promptly fired the first officer for incompetence and appointed twenty-two-year-old Alexander "Sandy" Anderson to fill that position. The crew members, according to one of the worried scientists assigned to the *Karluk*, had been hired from among available unemployed dock workers and were dubious at best. "One was a confirmed drug addict . . . another suffered from venereal disease; and in spite of orders that no liquor was to be carried, at least two smuggled supplies on board." One person was travelling under an alias, but there could have been more. None of them had Arctic experience. The crew had been hired for a routine round trip north but were unprepared for the hardships of overwintering in polar regions. They were, however, available to sign up on short notice and were willing to work for low wages. Many thought they would be back south before winter set in.

Discord was a passenger on board from the very beginning. The scientists expressed concerns about the adequacy of food provisions, warm clothing, and equipment. Without proper equipment like warm clothes and snow goggles, explorers could suffer from snow blindness and frostbite. Travel by dogsled was slow, arduous, and required frequent rest stops, even by mushers and dogs in top physical condition. Nutrition was vital to fend off scurvy, typhoid, or pneumonia. Stefansson, who was mostly absent on "other business" in the hectic weeks leading up to the sailing, revealed few expedition plans to his team and dismissed their concerns as "impertinent and disloyal." He espoused a simple diet philosophy: "My experience shows explorers had best live off the country. As far north as land has been discovered there is plenty of bear, caribou, muskox, seal and walrus. The provisions taken will be grains like rice and oats, and only dried fruit." As backup, tins of pemmican were loaded on board the *Karluk*.

Stefansson had other disagreements with the scientists. He saw himself as overall commander, but the Geological Survey of Canada, which had assigned four government scientists to the expedition, believed their work should be directed from Ottawa. Dr. R.M. Anderson, leader of the Southern Party, threatened to resign over Stefansson's claim to publication rights for all expedition writings. This was serious, because Anderson had the academic credentials Stefansson lacked. He was a respected scholar with an international reputation for thorough, detailed work, whereas Stefansson was seen as a self-promoting loose cannon who was more interested in photo ops than science.

The CAE scientists pose in front of the Empress Hotel in Victoria, June 1913. Front row (left to right): Wilkins (with camera), Chipman, Bartlett, Stefansson, Anderson, Murray. Back row (left to right): McKinlay (seated), Beuchat, Mamen, Jenness, Malloch, Cox, O'Neill, Johansen. LIBRARY AND ARCHIVES CANADA PA-074066

The CAE's international scientific team comprised some of the most distinguished men in their fields, but only two had previous polar experience: medical officer Alistair Forbes-Mackay and oceanographer James Murray had both accompanied Sir Ernest Shackleton's expedition to Antarctica from 1907 to 1909.

Among the younger scientists were William Laird McKinlay, a diminutive Scottish mathematics teacher nicknamed Wee Mac, whose position was magnetician/meteorologist, and Bjarne Mamen, a ski champion from Norway, who was taken on as topographer/forester, although he had no experience in the field.

There was a distinctive divide between the sailors crewing the *Karluk* and the scientists she carried on board. Each group stuck to their assigned tasks and did not mix, their separation based on social standing and education. More passengers, and about thirty sled dogs, would join them later along the Alaskan coast. Prior to departure, some of the crew members decided to search around the docks for a pet cat. Maritime superstition held that a cat would bring good luck. (A black cat would be an even better good-luck omen, contrary to the common belief that black cats brought bad luck.) Cats ate rodents, which could damage hemp rigging and food stores, and they created a sense of home for men away on long voyages. Cats had a keen sense of balance, which was important at sea, and once designated the official onboard feline, the cat was well treated because keeping it happy was certain to ensure fair weather. When Stefansson heard about the plan, he nixed it, saying the dogs would only eat the cat. But, just before sailing, one of the crew smuggled a scrawny, dirty, mostly black kitten below deck. They called her Nigeraurak, meaning "little black one" in the Inuit language (although when cleaned up, she revealed white feet and throat). She quickly became their mascot and was well fed and entertained, especially by Fred Maurer, the fireman. At first she was hidden in the foc's'le (forecastle, or crew living quarters in the ship's bow) but soon made her way aft, where she was the centre of attention as the men tried to teach her some tricks.

Trickier still was sorting out and finding room for all the expedition gear. Because there were two separate parties with two separate missions, Stefansson had purchased for $8,000, sight unseen, a small gas-powered schooner, the *Alaska*, to be used as the supply ship for the primarily land-based Southern Party. The 47-ton, 17.5-metre wooden ship, which had a 50-horsepower gas engine, had been built in Seattle in 1912 to carry US mail through the Bering Sea to Kotzebue, Alaska. In July 1913, Stefansson wired Ottawa from Nome, Alaska, that the *Karluk* and the *Alaska* were both overloaded with expedition equipment and recommended another schooner be purchased as backup in Nome rather than at the old whaling station on Herschel Island, as originally planned. His telegram stated, "Many excellent gas schooners for sale cheap, account hard times." He got the go-ahead and bought the wooden schooner *Mary Sachs* for $5,000. She was ready to sail the next day to serve as a tender shuttling people and supplies to expedition campsites and conducting oceanographic work on Arctic currents. As they set off together, the men dubbed their little three-ship flotilla the "Expedition Navy."

In the confusion surrounding preparations for the expedition, men and their equipment were separated and ended up on different ships. Equipment and supplies were piled high on the *Karluk*'s deck along with sacks of coal to feed her steam engine. Henri Beuchat and Diamond Jenness, anthropologists assigned to the Southern Party, found themselves on the *Karluk*, while their equipment was stowed on board the *Alaska*. McKinlay, also a Southern Party participant on board the *Karluk*, discovered most of his equipment, too, was on the *Alaska*. No need to worry, Stefansson assured them: everything would be resolved when all three ships reunited at their Herschel Island base off the northern Yukon coast in the Beaufort Sea. "Heaven help us all if we fail to reach Herschel Island," McKinlay wrote in his diary. In a letter posted to a friend in Boston about his new adventure, Bartlett wrote, "This will have the North Pole trip 'beaten to a frazzle.'" The day before departure, he sent a telegram to the deputy minister of Naval Service in Ottawa, informing him that the ship was "absolutely unsuitable to remain in winter ice."

CHAPTER

4

Under Way at Last

ON JUNE 17, 1913, HMCS *KARLUK* finally set sail from Victoria, BC, amid great fanfare. The official send-off featured speeches by Mayor Alfred J. Morley, Lieutenant Governor Thomas Wilson Patterson, and BC Premier Sir Richard McBride, who presented the expedition with new Canadian Red Ensign flags to be raised on newly discovered lands. The luncheons, dinners, ceremonies, and salutes for the scientists had gone on for weeks prior to the ship's departure. They were even given the keys to the city.

Cheering crowds gathered at the dock to wave bon voyage. A flotilla of harbour vessels blew their whistles in joyful support as the *Karluk* headed out and up the west coast to Alaska. It was late in the season to be starting a Far North voyage, and all they could hope for was good weather and calm seas.

Although strengthened for ice service, she was in no way the equivalent of Newfoundland's North Atlantic ships with which Bartlett was familiar. Instead of a steel-hulled icebreaking vessel, he had an old whaler that had been reinforced with crossbeams and extra sheathing. He had accepted this assignment under the assumption he would not have to overwinter in Arctic waters, and he was starting to have doubts about that belief. But it was too late to turn back. Stefansson disembarked in Esquimalt after the ceremonies were concluded to attend to more expedition business and work on a book he was writing about Arctic life. In his pocket, he had contracts with three international newspapers for a series of articles about his adventures. Stefansson took the opportunity to send a dispatch to the press informing them about his objectives for the expedition: "While every reasonable precaution will be taken to safeguard the lives of the party, it is realised both by the backers of the expedition and the members of it, that even the lives of the party are secondary to the accomplishment of the work." He rejoined the *Karluk* in Nome, Alaska, and sailed to the start of his northern explorations.

Bartlett had never sailed up the North Pacific coast to Alaska before and took great pleasure in watching the dramatic scenery—snow-capped mountains, glaciers, inlets, islands, and fjords. As they cruised through the

Inside Passage from June 18 to 23, the mood among the scientific passengers on board was relaxed. They adapted quickly to onboard life and lounged on the deck amid the sacks of coal and wooden crates. "Just think," one of them commented while sipping coffee, "this is a bonus. We get a sea trip to Nome, tobacco, good food, and all the comforts of home. Not only that, but we get paid for all this time on board." But as the *Karluk* navigated through the pristine waters, trouble started early. Both the engine and the steering mechanism required constant repair, but they kept going. On July 2, the ship reached the Bering Sea in foggy weather with increasingly colder temperatures. No longer could the passengers sit on deck without warmer clothing, even though the sun set at midnight and it was light at 3:00 AM.

Six days later, they made it to Nome and joined the *Alaska* and the *Mary Sachs*. Nome was a tiny coastal village that had sprung up with the discovery of gold; fishing, the fur trade, and reindeer herding kept the economy going after the gold ran out. It was the last point of civilization the expedition members would see before heading into the icy wilderness.

While the equipment was being sorted out and the ships were being loaded, the scientists demanded a meeting with Stefansson to discuss his plans for the Northern Party. (The Southern Party, under Dr. Anderson, had a much firmer understanding of their study mandate.) The meeting did not go well. Stefansson's dismissive attitude and refusal to divulge his survey plans offended many, and some of the men threatened to resign from the expedition. Others had read the press clippings in which Stefansson was quoted as saying the scientific work took precedence over staff safety and that they could very well be trapped in ice for most of the year. Still, even though many were alarmed at the turn of events, none left the expedition. Stefansson had counted on the scientists' professionalism and had been certain no staff members would defect, regardless of what he did.

* * *

Even with the extra ships, the *Karluk* was overloaded when she departed from Nome. Stefansson noted "she would never have been allowed to sail had there been at the port of Nome rigid inspectors unwilling to except an exploring vessel from the rules that were supposed to promote the safety of ships at sea." But no one said a word. Bartlett immediately directed all hands to prepare the ship and themselves before their voyage into the Arctic Ocean:

> We blew down the boiler, overhauled the engines, took on fresh water and rearranged our stores and equipment, so that we might know where everything was to be found. The weather was very variable . . . windy at times, with occasional showers. Some of the scientific staff went ashore and cut grass for use in our boots later on; when a man is wearing

> the deerskin boots so essential in Arctic work, it is necessary for him to line the bottom with dry grass to act as a cushion for his feet as he walks over the rough sea ice and also to absorb the perspiration, for otherwise his feet would be in constant danger of freezing.

Just north of Nome, twenty-eight sled dogs were taken on board. Nigeraurak no longer had free run of the ship. On July 27, the *Karluk* crossed over the Arctic Circle; Bartlett jokingly asked the men if they had felt the bump. Just off the north coast of Alaska, they encountered the worst summer ice in local memory. It was a serious obstacle, but Stefansson urged Bartlett to press on along the coast toward Herschel Island with all due speed. Bartlett knew the ship would never survive the greater crushing power of ice near land compared to that in the open ocean, but it was no use trying to change Stefannson's mind: he would not be convinced to take a different route. Ultimately, Bartlett took independent action and steered the *Karluk* away from land and into open water, looking for sea lanes north.

Once they had passed through Bering Strait, the scientific team spent little time on academic work: they were too busy wondering what would happen next. The year 1913 was an especially bad one for Arctic navigation, and the *Karluk* hit very rough seas. Cabins were flooded, clothing and papers were soaked. Many of the men were miserable with seasickness.

Robert Bartlett, captain of the CAE flagship, *Karluk*, on deck with his trademark pipe.

LIBRARY AND ARCHIVES CANADA C-025962

Sooner than anticipated, more loose ice began appearing, growing thicker and thicker. Then they were stopped by a large, unbroken sheet of ice. Bartlett recalled that this was similar to the ice he had seen in Melville Bay on the west coast of Greenland: "It was part of the past season's ice. Seldom over a foot thick, it was honeycombed with water-holes. The *Roosevelt* could have plowed her way through it but the *Karluk* was powerless to do so." By mid-August, Bartlett was doubtful they would make it to their base at Herschel Island, a former whaling station and North West Mounted Police post since 1903. McKinlay was more positive, writing in his diary that "whatever defects she had, *Karluk* was proving herself a fine sea-boat."

When they reached the small Inuit settlement of Point Hope, two Inuit hunters, Pauyuraq ("Jerry") and Asecaq ("Jimmy") joined the ship. The next day, the permanent Arctic ice pack was spotted, much earlier than expected. Bartlett faced it head on, but after several attempts to break through, he was forced to back off. Then, about forty kilometres from Point Barrow, a headland on the north coast of Alaska that separates the Chukchi Sea on the west from the Beaufort Sea on the east, the *Karluk* successfully shoved a passageway into the ice but, without sufficient power to maintain forward momentum, became trapped. Stefansson disembarked to walk over the floes toward Point Barrow. The *Karluk* drifted eastward for three days locked in this frigid embrace. Reaching open water off Cape Smythe, near Point Hope, on August 6, she pulled in to pick up Stefansson, who was accompanied by his long-time friend John Hadley, a veteran trapper. (Hadley was entered into the ship's register with the occupation of carpenter.) Also coming on board were two more Inuit hunters, Kataktovik ("Claude") and Kuraluk, with his wife Kiruk ("Auntie"), who was to help with the cooking and sew sealskins for winter clothing as the voyage continued. With them were their two daughters, Helen (Qagguluk), aged eight, and Mugpi (Ruth), aged three.

At this time, the Inuit were subsistence hunters, and their knowledge of the land, how to navigate over barren terrain, and how to find food and build shelter was invaluable to European explorers with little appreciation of the hardships of Arctic life. The women's skills in preserving food and sewing warm, waterproof clothing from animal hides were also key to survival in these harsh conditions.

Bartlett was becoming more and more apprehensive about the extent of pack ice around them. He noted that the brass stem plates on the extreme front of the *Karluk*'s bow, extending from keel to forecastle deck, were already damaged. He was sure now that they would probably not make it to their Herschel Island winter port. In the next few days, Bartlett moved farther north and away from the coast by following open water channels that allowed him to move forward faster. The only scientific work that could be accomplished during this time was by oceanographer

James Murray, who dredged up diverse species of Arctic sea life and conducted regular depth soundings.

By August 13, Bartlett had calculated their position many times and come up with the same result each time: they were 378 kilometres east of Point Barrow, with an equivalent distance yet to go to reach Herschel Island. This was the farthest easterly point they would reach on their journey because, held fast in the icefield and unable to free herself, the *Karluk* started drifting backward to the west, stuck, as one crew member said, like a nut in the middle of frosty pudding.

By September 10, the ship and its hapless passengers had backtracked 161 kilometres to Point Barrow. "We were stuck so hard and fast in that ice 40 feet thick," Bartlett recalled, "that all the motor trucks in Canada couldn't have pulled us out." No further progress would be made in 1913, and the *Karluk* would have to overwinter in the ice. Reaching their winter port was not possible: they were trapped for the season. Fred Maurer, one of the firemen, wrote how "day after day and night after night we lay in helpless imprisonment" within the ship inside the icefield. Then things went from boring to terrifying. Blizzards and storms made the ice crack, buckle, rise up, and reform in grotesque shapes. McKinlay noted in his diary that "huge ice blocks larger than houses were being tossed about like pebbles." The *Karluk* could be crushed, along with everyone on board.

CHAPTER

5

Ice, Ice Everywhere

WITH THE *KARLUK* ICEBOUND OFF the mouth of Colville River near Cape Halkatt, Alaska, and not going anywhere, Stefansson professed to be concerned about the need for fresh meat to sustain them throughout their captivity and to prevent scurvy. On September 19, the man who stated they were "well provisioned for three years and . . . the supplies could be eked out to cover four years" announced he was forming a hunting party to forage for caribou and other game around Colville River. This came as a surprise to Bartlett, because Stefansson had earlier told him caribou were nearly extinct in that area. And Stefansson was taking with him the two Inuit hunters, Pauyuraq and Asecaq, plus some staff who were clearly not trackers, shooters, or butchers: his personal secretary Burt McConnell, photographer George Wilkins, and anthropologist Diamond Jenness. He also chose the twelve best dogs to pull the sleds, which were loaded with a substantial amount of supplies from the ship's stores.

Bartlett was informed they would be back to the ship in ten days "if no accident happens" and was handed a letter in which Stefansson had written instructions about his responsibilities during the absence should the ship begin to move again: "Send a party ashore, to erect one or more beacons giving information of the ship's whereabouts."

September 23 brought a fierce northeast gale with high winds, snow, and dense fog. As if this was not terrifying enough for those on board, the ice floe that still had the *Karluk* immobilized in it broke away from the main mass. It picked up speed, accelerating rapidly to almost ninety-seven kilometres a day, but travelling to the west, not to the east. Poor visibility made it difficult for Bartlett to accurately calculate the ship's position. The rate of drift was much faster than Bartlett or Stefansson had expected. By early October, the *Karluk* was off Point Barrow and drifting off course way out into deep water. Stefansson later said he believed the storm had freed the ship, allowing her to make progress to the east and rendezvous with her sister ships the *Alaska* and the *Mary Sachs* and the rest of the expedition. Clearly, he and his party would not be rejoining Bartlett and the other scientists, who were well aware they had been abandoned.

Occasionally, the ice would fracture and cracks would appear in the floe close to the ship. The men would try to free the *Karluk* by using iron bars, pickaxes, and long-handled augers to break up the ice around the hull. The sides were cleared so that if the ice began to press together, then perhaps the ship would be able to rise up onto it and not be crushed.

Powering forward at full speed had no effect on breaking up the ice. It was thick and solid and remained cemented to the sides of the ship, which continued to drift with the ocean currents. Most troubling of all was when they could hear the ice floes grinding against each other. "Ice rafting" also occurred when pack ice collided, pushing the edge of one floe up to override another until the height mounded above the top deck.

Nor was the weather helpful: whiteouts and sub-zero temperatures continued to be the norm. Although the scientists tried to remain optimistic and occupy themselves with preparations for their Arctic studies, they became increasingly frustrated and apprehensive. Everyone worried about where they were being taken and whether it would be possible to break free, even in the spring. One of two things would happen: either the pack ice would thaw and free the *Karluk*, or it would consolidate and crush her—and them.

Whatever might happen, they still had to eat now. Bartlett and the Inuit hunters set out over the ice on snowshoes to some of the open sea lanes and water holes in order to shoot seals and ducks. Bjarne Mamen had an even better idea: the former ski champion showed them how they could cover more distance and go faster on skis than on snowshoes. Bartlett gave it a try and was won over by his new mode of transport.

When they shot birds, the new ice that had formed in the open channels (or "leads") made it difficult to recover their kills. They came up with an ingenious solution. Bartlett recalled, "We broke off a piece of thicker ice large enough to hold a man, and standing on it as on a raft, would push along with our ski-poles and work around to pick up the birds." Salt water, he explained, does not freeze as easily as fresh water, but when it does freeze, the ice is much tougher and less brittle than freshwater ice.

Meanwhile, some scientific work continued. McKinlay installed an anemometer, a device for measuring wind speed, and mounted it high up in the rigging on the edge of the crow's nest, where it would catch everything from a gentle breeze to a ferocious blast. The wires ran down the mast and along the deck into McKinlay's cabin, where he noted readings on an indicator dial.

James Murray had been dredging the bottom for some days and now brought up a small octopus. This was a surprise catch compared to the round, smooth stones and pebbles he had usually retrieved. Then he began to recover specimens of previously unknown sea creatures. In one day, he had collected eleven different species. All were carefully catalogued.

The ship started leaking, and the men took turns manually pumping her out. It was hard work that consumed up to two hours every day. As one seaman wryly observed, what else did they have to do with their time? Ordinarily, they would have used steam power from the engine to do the pumping, but it had been shut down for more maintenance.

Although stuck fast in the ice floe, the *Karluk* did move. She shuddered and groaned continuously as fierce gusts of wind up to 129 kilometres per hour buffeted her rigging, and grinding ice chunks squeezed her hull. The passengers huddled close to the coal-fired stove in the lounge and tried to read by lantern light. Others went to their cabins and crawled into their narrow bunks, covering themselves with blankets to keep warm. But even a pillow pressed over their ears could not dampen the mournful sounds all around. Outside, there was no respite from the eternal grey as huge snowdrifts formed up and over the top deck. Bartlett ordered some of the crew to take shovels and bank up snow on the starboard side of the ship to act as insulation and make the interior as comfortable as possible. *Karluk* had become a ghost ship in a frozen snowscape.

Ice conditions off the north coast of Alaska were relentless in 1913, and the *Karluk* was only one of many ships that became trapped. The two smaller schooners of the Expedition Navy, which had shallower draft configurations, were able to navigate closer in to shore as far as Collinson Point, Alaska, where they overwintered. As winter set in and daylight grew shorter, the *Karluk* and her helpless passengers continued to drift west into the Arctic Ocean, hundreds of kilometres from land. By the end of November, they were approaching the Siberian Sea.

Stefansson and his party never came back to the ship, leaving behind twenty-two men, one woman, and two children helpless to do anything but wait for rescue or death. He never did locate the *Karluk*, nor did he exert any time or effort trying. His six-man group trekked to Point Barrow and then on to meet the Southern Party at Collinson Point, where Stefansson was quick to send off a newspaper article about his adventures but not to form a search party to find the *Karluk*. He formed a new Northern Party and spent the next five years, not just the initial three-year expedition time frame, exploring the North on foot and attempting to commandeer additional supplies from the Southern Party (which continued its mission until 1916).

CHAPTER

6

Death Throes

BY THE FIRST WEEK OF NOVEMBER, the sun barely shone until noon. By mid-November, there was no daylight at all. The solid Arctic night would be with them for the next two and a half months. This was beyond depressing. Ernest Chafe, the mess steward, commented that "so long as the sun was with us to measure the night and day, it was not so bad. But when the orb disappeared, a sort of sickening sensation of loneliness came over us." That loneliness was to be their constant companion.

Late in 1913, the *Karluk* was in Russian waters, closer to Siberia than Alaska. Still the inexorable westward drift persisted. For five months, she had been trapped among massive fields of ice ridges, drifting farther and farther off course. Prisoners on board, the passengers continued to occupy their time with hunting and reinforcing winter clothing, especially footwear. Their stockpile of food was supplemented with more seal meat. Bartlett estimated they had accumulated 41 seals, about 25 kilograms, enough to last 25 people 67 days. "Not everyone on board liked seal meat," he observed, "but all could eat it."

As the temperature dropped to -34C° and high winds drove the snow sideways through the endless Arctic night, Bartlett remained stoic. "I made up my mind that we were in the place where all the bad weather was manufactured, to be passed along to Medicine Hat and thence distributed to Chicago and Boston and points south." At the time, they were just eighty kilometres north of rocky Herald Island, which lay sixty kilometres east of Wrangel Island. Some thought they could see land on the distant horizon. On clear nights, they were amazed by displays of the aurora borealis, the northern lights, as they changed from a diffuse glow to arcs that hung like curtains of red and green in the black sky.

December 21, the winter solstice, was the day for which all of them had been waiting. Now darkness would be slowly retreating and daylight would be coming back, little by little. Bartlett kept a close eye on the mood of his passengers, and as the December holidays approached, he noted, "Now that they were in the neighbourhood of the place where Santa Claus came from, they seemed determined to observe the day in a manner worthy of the jolly old saint."

In spite of the gloomy outlook, Christmas was celebrated out on the ice with decorations, presents, and games, followed by a feast. Describing their Christmas Day festivities in his memoir, Bartlett wrote:

> At six o'clock on Christmas morning the second engineer [Robert Williamson] and McKinlay started in decorating the cabin with the flags of the International Code and a fine lot of colored ribbon which Mr. Hadley had brought with him from Point Barrow for the trading he had hoped to do in Banks Land. Later in the morning I went around and distributed presents to the Eskimo[s]. I gave each of the Eskimo men a hunting-knife and a watch and the Eskimo woman a cotton dress, stockings and underwear, talcum powder, soap, a looking-glass, a comb and brush and some ribbon, with a cotton dress for each of the little girls. At eleven o'clock the first event on our type-written programme began—the sports. This was the list:
>
> *D.G.S. Karluk. Xmas Day, 1913*
> The events of the sports programme arranged for the day will take place in the following order:
>
> 1. 100 yards sprint
> 2. Long jump (standing)
> 3. Long jump (running)
> 4. Sack race
> 5. High jump
>
> Interval for refreshments
>
> 6. Three-legged race
> 7. Putting the weight
> 8. 50-yard burst

9. Hop, step and leap
10. Tug of war
11. Obstacle race
12. Wrestling

Proceedings will commence at 11 AM (*Karluk* time); dogs and bookmakers not allowed on the field.

The doctor was umpire and wore a paper rosette.

Dinner as usual was at half past four. I confess that I felt homesick and thought of other Christmas dinners. It was my fourth Christmas in the Arctic; in 1898 I had been with Peary at Cape D'Urville on the *Windward* and in 1905 and 1908 at Cape Sheridan with the *Roosevelt*, but our situation now had far more elements of uncertainty in it than we had felt on those occasions and in addition this time it was I who had the responsibility for the lives and fortunes of every man, woman and child in the party.

We sat down at 4:30 PM to a menu laid out and typewritten by McKinlay:

"Such a bustle ensued"
Mixed Pickles Sweet Pickles
Oyster Soup
Lobster
Bear Steak
Ox Tongue
Potatoes Green Peas
Asparagus and Cream Sauce
Mince Pie Plum Pudding
Mixed Nuts
Tea Cake
Strawberries

"God Bless You, Merry Gentlemen;
May Nothing You Dismay!"

> Murray [James, oceanographer] produced a cake which had been given in Victoria to cut for this particular occasion and which he had kept carefully secreted in his cabin. Dinner, which was a great credit to Bob [Templeman], the cook, was followed by cigars and cigarettes and a concert on the Victrola which had been presented to the ship by Sir Richard McBride. We had records that played both classical and popular music, vocal and instrumental, and we kept this up with singing, to a late hour. Malloch [George Stewart, geologist] wrote a Christmas letter of many pages to his father.

For once, the crew, the scientists, and the Inuit family all seemed to enjoy each other's company. Although alcohol was not allowed on board, there was a small stash under lock and key to be used for medicinal purposes and on very special occasions. Bartlett passed around a bottle of whisky, and all the glasses were filled. The last time they had any whisky was when they crossed the Arctic Circle or when Dr. Forbes-Mackay prescribed it for seasickness. Bartlett even put a small amount into his own glass, though he was a teetotaller. (When asked once why he abstained, he had answered, "Because God gave me my body and I propose to take care of it.") This was, after all, a special occasion, and an exception would be made. He asked everyone to stand and, in a sombre tone, proposed a toast: "To the loved ones back home." No one said a word. Silently, they all raised their glasses, drank, and sat down again. Thoughts turned to friends and family and the familiar Christmas traditions they had enjoyed in previous years and hoped to enjoy again.

On December 29, land was again visible in the distance, but it was unclear whether it was Wrangel Island or its smaller neighbour, Herald Island. Perhaps they would not be confined to the ship much longer. The crew took depth soundings that indicated twenty-five fathoms (forty-six metres) of water beneath the *Karluk*. The problem was that these readings did not correlate with the navigation charts on board. Bartlett's chronometer readings told him it was Herald Island. He climbed aloft for a better look, but because of the poor light, it looked distorted, like a big mirage on the horizon.

As the new year approached and spirits sank even lower, the men tried to distract themselves by organizing a sporting event and celebrating a new start in 1914. Bells were used on board ships to regulate a sailor's duty watch, one for each half-hour of a four-hour watch. The traditional sixteen bells were struck at midnight on December 31—eight for the old year and eight for the new. At the striking of the last bell, McKinlay observed the custom by parading up and down the *Karluk*'s deck, "raising the devil with the dinner bell." Then all the passengers congregated in the lounge to toast, with juice or leftover whisky, the coming year and express hope for safe passage out of the ice. Then they marked the occasion with recitations of poetry by Scottish lyricist Robert Burns and a loud, if off-key, rendition of "Auld Lang Syne." Captain Bartlett remained in his cabin, thinking about the limited options for saving his ship and his charges.

For New Year's Day, they organized a soccer match. It was Team Scotland versus Team All Nations. For a whistle, they improvised with a harmonica, but referee Bartlett had to stop blowing it; the temperature was so cold that it froze to his lips and peeled the skin off. For the ball, Bartlett described a creation "made of seal-gut cut into sections and sewed up with surgeon's plaster over the seams. We blew it up with a pipe stem and plugged up the hole. To protect the ball we had a sealskin casing made to fit it; the result was a fairly good ball, constructed on the same principle as any college ball." They played on a regulation-size field marked out on smooth new ice, which was about half a metre thick. Goalposts were placed at each end. Coffee was served at halftime. The final score: All Nations 8, Scotland 3.

After New Year's, when all hands had resolved to remain optimistic in the upcoming year, the ice began cracking. It formed huge pressure ridges composed of ice fragments piled up in a line, with the steep-sloped ridges rising up as much as three metres above adjacent stretches of level ice. Over the next few days, wrote McKinlay, "the twanging, drumming, ominous ice sounds got louder and nearer." Ice ground against the hull, especially around the engine room, subjecting it to enormous force. As a precaution against the possibility that the lanterns on board might cause an accidental fire, Bartlett ordered some of the supplies offloaded onto the ice and placed inside a hastily constructed shelter of crates. His intention was also to lighten the load and keep the *Karluk* sitting higher in the ice to reduce pressure on her hull.

Tea was packed into tin containers, and cooking pots were fashioned from gasoline canisters. Biscuits were crammed into boxes, and .22-calibre cartridges were placed in waterproof packets. Kerosene was decanted into smaller cans. Everything that could be was downsized because if they were forced to travel by sled, they could not haul large heavy objects.

Hadley checked and reinforced the sleds, and they kept working on stitching tighter seams on their sealskin boots and parkas. Every man prepared a knapsack of his personal items—valuables, papers, dry clothing, and tobacco—that he could grab quickly if he had to abandon ship. Rationing of foodstuffs became necessary, so coffee, tea, cocoa, and milk became merely coloured water. Food was served almost raw to conserve on fuel. The fresh, frozen seal meat and blubber, high in Vitamin C, was a daily staple to help prevent scurvy. The rich food eaten at Christmas and New Year's was now only a fond memory.

The men spent hours working in the dark, shifting crates from the deck down the gangway of packed snow and onto the surrounding ice. It was dangerous work. They could not see where they were putting their feet—into slushy depressions in the ice or onto ice fragments that would tip over under their weight and send them crashing down on their

Close-up view of the *Karluk*'s bow locked in pack ice. LIBRARY AND ARCHIVES CANADA C-071058

knees. Over on the big floe, they made a snow igloo and built a house of stacked boxes with wooden boards for a floor and then brought in a Primus stove. Still, this was only an emergency shelter, just in case.

On the night of January 10, 1914, the *Karluk* was still stuck in ice when the ominous sound of the ship's stern being ripped open by shifting pack ice was heard by all on board. A loud bang pierced the air. It sounded like the firing of a cannon. She was breaking apart. They heard splitting wood and crashing beams from the engine room as, squeezed in a vise-like grip, bottom and side timbers splintered, and pipes and pumps broke apart. A jagged frozen mass had punched a three-metre hole in the vessel's hull, while the unrelenting external pressure slowly squeezed the life out of the *Karluk*. The heavy ice had fractured her spine and broken her ribs.

Captain Bartlett later recalled the moment:

> I was awakened by a loud report like a rifle shot. I heard a splitting, crashing sound. Then there came a tremor and quiver all through the ship. We could hear water rushing into the hold and by lantern light could see it pouring in at different places. It would be useless to attempt to rig a temporary pump; the break was beyond repair.

Cradled in the surrounding pack ice, the *Karluk* remained upright as the men now worked furiously to salvage as much as possible. Provisions, fuel, scientific equipment, personal possessions, ten thousand pounds of pemmican, and excited, barking dogs were all dumped outside.

But nobody could find the cat. In all the noise and activity, the cat had disappeared. The next morning, as the ship was still upright but filling fast with water, Nigeraurak appeared and was quickly scooped up into a basket. She was delivered into one of the makeshift shelters on the ice. Inside, the two girls were excited to play with their feline companion; the cat was not so pleased.

In the late afternoon of January 11, 1914, after five months stuck in sea ice, the *Karluk* was on the move: she was going down. McKinlay dedicated a large entry in his diary describing Bartlett and the death of the *Karluk*:

> He had a huge fire roaring in the galley stove, and he had moved the gramophone in with the full stock of records. He played them one by one, throwing each record as it ended into the galley fire. He found Chopin's *Funeral March* [Piano Sonata No. 2 in B-flat minor, Op. 35], played it over and laid it aside. He was really very comfortable, eating when he felt like it and drinking plenty of coffee and tea. There was just enough ice pressure to keep the ship from sinking . . . All day the Captain remained on board. For hours nothing changed. The ship was full of water and only prevented from sinking by the grip of the ice . . . Then at 3:15 a shout, "She's going!" brought everyone onto the ice. The *Karluk* was settling down at the bow. As the minutes went by, the deck sank almost entirely under water. Captain Bartlett put the *Funeral March* on the Victrola. With the water running along the starboard side of the deck and pouring down the hatches, he waited at the rail until it came down level with the ice. Then he stepped off. The *Karluk* slowly settled by the bow and sank gradually into 38 fathoms [70 metres] of water. Captain Bartlett, deeply moved, stood right alongside her until she was gone.

As Captain Bartlett had remained on board, distraught but resigned to the impending loss of the ship under his command, water rose in the cabin, and escape became imperative. He had to leave and whispered his final "goodbye."

He later said that on the night of January, 10, 1914, he felt her heel and knew the end was near. "The men worked steadily and without a sign of fear. A couple of bottles of whisky used judiciously in their coffee helped a whole lot."

> We had a lot of records, and when I felt her going, I got out Chopin's *Funeral March* and put that on. I also put out all the flags as she may as well have a decent funeral. Then I got off and stood on the ice and watched her. Down she went, head first, stern up in the air, and the phonograph going. It was a tragic moment. It was like losing a dear friend. I remembered hearing about Admiral Cervera down in Santiago [Cuba] when his ship was lost so I took off my hood, and as the ship went down, I said like him: "Adios, *Karluk*."

This was not the first time Bartlett had had a ship sink under him. He had been shipwrecked twice before, both times on the southern coast of Newfoundland. Although the feeling was not new, it was still emotional. The *Karluk* had been home for months. "Yet I could feel no despair in our present situation," he recalled, "for we had comfortable quarters on a floe which was practically indestructible and plenty of food and fuel, so that with patience, perseverance, courage and good fortune we should be able to win our way safety in due time." Others might have disagreed with such an optimistic outlook.

The day after the *Karluk* sank, mess steward Ernest Chafe described the place where she had disappeared as "completely frozen over and every trace of the ship obliterated." Sleeping in the igloo or in the box-house of crates on the ice, the occupants could not relax or snuggle into their sleeping bags. If the ice cracked and a lead of open water appeared, as it often did, they would need to have their arms free to swim to safety. One night, a one-metre crack opened up right down the middle of one of the shelters. "In a few seconds," McKinlay wrote in his diary, "there was a lane of water just where two people had been sleeping." The shipwrecked group stranded on the ice consisted of twenty-two men, one woman, two children, sixteen dogs, and one cat. With everyone accounted for, what would they do next?

CHAPTER

7

Shipwreck Camp Moves Out

BARTLETT IMMEDIATELY TOOK PERSONAL RESPONSIBILITY for the well-being of the *Karluk*'s woeful survivors. Their most immediate need was to maintain a warm shelter. It was the middle of the Arctic winter and dark from the middle of November to the end of January. It was -40° in both the Celsius and Fahrenheit temperature scales. Bartlett knew travelling over the ice under those conditions was dangerous, even for experienced polar survivalists. And he knew his group was certainly not experienced. He decided to wait until mid-February, when daylight would begin to return, before moving out. But where could they go? Which way was land? Bartlett calculated their best chance was to travel south for solid land on Wrangel Island off the coast of

Siberia. It would be an arduous journey, but remaining on the ice waiting for rescue would be certain death. Nobody knew where they were, and no ship would be breaking through the pack ice in winter. They would use the intervening time to get ready to save themselves.

Already they had the beginnings of a cozy settlement. Bartlett recalled, "I had the Eskimo build a large snow igloo on the floe near where we had our box-house of supplies, to furnish additional shelter for ourselves and the dogs. We began making wooden boxes for the protection of our Primus stoves." A tent was erected to store an eclectic selection of essentials salvaged from the *Karluk* such as:

70 suits of Jaeger underwear
3 dozen wool shirts
200 pairs of stockings
6 fleece suits
4 Burberry hunting suits
2 large sacks of waterskin boots [sealskin boots that shed water]
100 pairs of mukluks
100 fawn skins
12 hair-seal skins
20 reindeer skins
50 Jaeger blankets
20 mattresses
250 sacks of coal
33 cases of gasoline
4,056 lbs [1,840 kilograms] of Underwood pemmican

5,222 lbs [2,369 kilograms] of Hudson's Bay pemmican
3 drums of coal oil
2 boxes of tea
200 tins of milk
250 lbs [113 kilograms] of sugar
2 boxes of chocolate
2 boxes of butter
1 box of cocoa
3 large cases of codfish
4 cases of desiccated eggs
114 cases of pilot bread [hardtack biscuits]
5 barrels of beef
9 sledges, each capable of carrying 600-700 lbs [272–318 kilograms]
2,000 board feet of lumber
3 coal stoves
2 wood stoves
90 ft [27 metres] of stove-pipe
1 extra suit of sails
2 wooden Peterborough canoes
2 sewing machines
candles, lanterns and matches

To Bartlett, this list was a testament to how well they were supplied with all the provisions necessary to survive in the Arctic. They were, he said, "like the Swiss Family Robinson, well equipped for comfortable living, waiting until the return of the sun should give us daylight enough for ice travel."

After his thirty-six hours of non-stop work directing operations to protect the band of survivors from the elements, a fatigued Bob Bartlett turned in and slept for twelve hours straight. The temperature, he recalled "was not severe, just -40°F and the nearest land, Wrangel Island, only about 80 miles [129 kilometres] away." Morale remained high because the marooned shipmates knew their captain had come through perilous maritime situations before and was an expert in polar survival. Bivouacked on what was for the time being a solid ice floe, they had assembled their igloo, lean-to, tents, food, fuel, rifles, sledges, and dogs into a settlement appropriately dubbed "Shipwreck Camp."

The snow igloo was five metres long by four metres wide, with wooden rafters and a canvas roof. The box-house was eight metres long by six metres wide, banked up all around the outside with snow to block drafts. One end of the box-house was partitioned to create the galley area, with a stove, where the cook, Robert Templeman, would have a place to work. The kitchen equipment was assembled using components rescued from the *Karluk*'s engine room. The shelters were surrounded by a perimeter of barrels, crates, and bags of coal also from the engine room. As on the ship, much of their time was spent sewing more fur clothing, skin-boots, and sleeping bags that they would need for the eventual march to Wrangel Island. Fur clothing was so thick and heavy that it had to be stitched by hand, but much of the other work could be done on sewing machines, and they had saved two from the *Karluk*. One was in the box-house and the other in the igloo; Kiruk operated one and chief engineer John Munro the other. (Munro had been a junior officer in the British Navy, and Bartlett found that he had a number of useful talents.) Kiruk and Munro also made canvas covers for the supplies that would be piled onto the sledges. None of this work would be possible once they were on the move toward land.

* * *

The ice drift was slowly carrying them and their camp in a southwest direction, but it was still too dark to set out. They would stay put, live off the supplies they had salvaged from the *Karluk*, and wait out winter until daylight lasted longer and an advance party could establish some supply bases along the projected route.

They followed a daily schedule much like they'd maintained on board ship while drifting. It was lights out at 10:00 PM. The night watchman was responsible for keeping the fires going and waking up the cook at 6:00 AM. There was time for games of cards or chess and occasionally a few songs around the stoves in the centre of their dwellings. A number of books had been saved from the *Karluk*'s library, and some caught up on their classical reading. There was *Wuthering Heights*, *Villette*, and *Jane Eyre*, plus more recent novels. Bartlett's constant companion was the *Rubaiyat of Omar Khayyam*, which he had received as a gift in 1901 and which he reread and found new meaning in every time he did so. Its pages were dog-eared and stuck together with tape along the spine. It had accompanied him on voyages from his apprenticeship training to his voyages with Peary, as well as every hunting and sealing trip.

In addition to their literary endeavours, the ship-wrecked company kept records of wind and weather, depth soundings, and temperature, which stalled in the -30s for days on end. But not everyone was happy with life at Shipwreck Camp and the decision to wait before setting off. Resentments began to fester.

Bartlett sent out small scouting teams of men across the ice to hunt for fresh meat and to establish a chain of food caches for the planned journey to Wrangel Island. Not all of those in his care were capable of strenuous sledging, and they could not carry everything they needed for the entire trip on the sledges they had. The first party, which consisted of the *Karluk*'s first and second mates, Sandy Anderson and Charles Barker, and two crewmen, John Brady and Edmund Golightly, with Bjarne Mamen as their scout, departed on January 20. In addition to stashing supplies at regular intervals and blazing a trail with flattened empty pemmican cans stuck to pinnacles of ice, four of the men would take the sledges and dogs farther and set up an advance base camp near Berry Point, on the north shore of Wrangel Island. They had a full range of supplies to last for three months, including full tins of pemmican. Along with biscuits and tea, Bartlett had lived off pemmican as an Arctic staple for 120 days at a time and "found it amply sufficient." It wasn't cordon bleu fare, but it sustained life. The Canadian Arctic Expedition had been issued two types of pemmican—one for humans, consisting of beef, raisins, sugar, and suet, all cooked together and then pressed and packed into blue tins, and a second kind for dogs, without the raisins and sugar, packed in red tins. The red or blue sheets of tin stood out against the white background for up to three kilometres and were positioned so as to clearly indicate the trail, open water, or a fissure.

Bartlett believed that small, desolate Herald Island lay about eighty kilometres south of Shipwreck Camp and that larger Wrangel Island was sixty kilometres west of Herald. Mamen would not accompany the party all the way but would return to Shipwreck Camp with a map of the trail and initial supply caches. He returned, but with a lacerated knee and dislocated kneecap from slipping down an ice ridge and falling on shards that cut to the bone. Dr. Forbes-Mackay dressed the wound, but second engineer Robert Williamson had the job of sliding the kneecap back into place every time it popped out.

The four-man advance party actually reached Herald Island, as was later discovered. The problem was that they never left. Perhaps because of ice moving quickly on ocean currents and treacherous sections of open water, they were stranded there. Maybe they had fallen through thin ice and drowned. Possibly accident or bloodshed had taken their lives. Or, were they confused and believed they had reached

Wrangel Island and would soon be joined by the main group? In any event, they were never seen again. It was not until ten years later that the mystery of their whereabouts would be solved.

On January 25, the sun peeked above the horizon for the first time in months and buoyed Shipwreck Camp's internees. They celebrated by digging up two cases of canned oysters discovered in the supply tent [and evidently overlooked in the supply list] and having the cook prepare a version of oyster stew for the evening meal.

Four members of the group did not want to wait any longer to set out. Dr. Alistair Forbes-Mackay of Edinburgh, oceanographer James Murray of Glasgow, anthropologist Dr. Henri Beuchat of Paris, and able seaman Stanley Morris from Caerwys, Wales, decided to leave early and travel directly over the sea ice to the Siberian coast. Forbes-Mackay and Murray had accompanied Shackleton on his Antarctic expedition of 1907–09 and had crossed the land ice near the South Pole. They felt they could handle these extreme northern conditions and shifting sea ice.

To the scientists, Bartlett did not look, or act, like a commander of men. Instead of a uniform, he had dressed, even before the *Karluk* sank, in a baggy sweater and loose pants. His demeanour was more collegial than authoritarian; he was just a fisherman, not a naval officer. That he appeared so to the scientists did not come as any surprise to Bartlett, who was well aware of their grumbling and second-guessing of his decisions. In any case, he had no control over these academics. They had been selected by Stefansson and worked under his direction. Bartlett, however, was responsible for the crew and tried to dissuade Stanley Morris by telling him that the splitting and shifting northern ice was totally different from the Antarctic ice Forbes-Mackay and Murray had experienced. But Morris was in awe of the scientists, so Bartlett relented and gave him permission to accompany them. Maybe, he reasoned, the strong, young Morris could be useful to the older men on their journey over the ice.

The four men were eager to get started, so Bartlett equipped them with a sledge and sufficient supplies for a fifty-day trip. He offered them their share of the dogs, but they refused, saying they preferred to haul the sledge themselves. In return, they had already signed a document that stated:

> We, the undersigned, in consideration of the present critical situation, desire to make an attempt to reach the land. We ask you to assist us by issuing to us from the general stores all necessary sledging and camping provisions and equipment for the proposed journey as per separate requisition already handed to you. On the understanding that you do so and continue as heretofore to supply us with our proportional share of provisions while we remain in camp, and in the event of our finding it necessary to return to the camp, we declare that we undertake the journey on our own initiative and absolve you from any responsibility whatever in the matter.

Reaffirming that this was solely their initiative and absolving him of any responsibility for the consequences of their decision, they handed the note to Bartlett. In response, he told the men that if for any reason they wanted to return to and rejoin the group, they were welcome to do so.

They left Shipwreck Camp on February 5. Ten days later, a scouting party under Ernest Chafe returning to camp came upon Forbes-Mackay, Morris, and Murray. In spite of fatigue and the loss of some of their provisions, which had fallen through an opening in the ice, they refused all advice to return to camp. Their clothes were damp, and Morris had a deep cut on his hand that looked infected. Still, they were going to move forward to solid ground. Beuchat was bringing up the rear and, in Chafe's opinion, appeared to be suffering from hypothermia and was having trouble breathing. His hands were so frostbitten that they had turned black and swollen and would no longer fit into his fur-lined mitts. He, too, resisted all pleas to turn around.

When the scouting party got back to camp, Chafe told Bartlett about the encounter. There was nothing they could do, so they continued preparations to move out with the *Karluk* survivors. Forbes-Mackay, Morris, Murray, and Beuchat were never heard from again. They may have been crushed by shifting ice floes or fallen through into open water. Like the *Karluk*, they were no more.

Bartlett's main group now consisted of eight *Karluk* crew members: John Munro (chief engineer), Robert Williamson (second engineer), Fred Maurer and George Breddy (firemen), Hugh Williams (seaman), Bob Templeman (cook), Ernest Chafe (mess steward), and the carpenter, John Hadley. Three scientists were still alive: William Laird McKinlay (magnetician), Bjarne Mamen (topographer), George Malloch, (geologist), and five Inuit (the family of four, and Kataktovik). Hadley, almost sixty years old, along with Bartlett and the Inuit were the only ones with experience travelling long distances over Arctic ice. These seventeen survivors were as ready as they would ever be to leave Shipwreck Camp.

No one wanted to abandon the cat, so Maurer and Hadley made a little drawstring bag from a piece of deerskin into which she was stuffed for travel. Sometimes she rode on top of a sled, and other times Maurer hung the bag around his neck, where she and he could share body heat inside his winter parka. Each night, after an igloo had been hastily constructed, they let her out of her bag and she would curl up to sleep among their gear or in a sealskin boot. Everyone pitched in to share some food scraps with Nigeraurak.

The dogs were doing fairly well, too: after they were fed, they curled up outside, nose to tail, and were soon covered with a blanket of snow.

The initial plan had been to head for Herald Island and use that as a staging area to get to Wrangel Island. Bartlett decided to break his large group into two smaller segments for travel. Each team would have sledges and dogs. But some of the dogs were weak, and he had lost others to fighting.

The men had to pitch in and help by hauling some of the heavily laden sledges. They carried enough supplies for sixty days (divided among them) and would supplement with the supplies stashed along the way and any seals they might kill.

The first team left on February 19 under the direction of Chafe, Hadley, and McKinlay. Bartlett himself led the last team out of Shipwreck Camp on February 24. They had three komatiks (sledges with wooden runners and cross-bars lashed together with rawhide), which were handled by Kataktovik, Kuraluk, and Bartlett. They could not bring everything with them, so had to leave behind two tons of food and most of their fuel. On the remote chance the camp should drift into inhabited waters, or be spotted by Native hunters, Bartlett left behind a note in a copper drum stating their location when the *Karluk* sank and their projected route to Wrangel Island. Bartlett brought his nautical charts. With ice drift, the distance to Wrangel was estimated at sixty-four kilometres, but the journey proved to be twice that distance.

The trip was hellish. The ice surface was now breaking up, making travel slow and difficult. At first, the parties were able to travel along the trail marked out by Anderson's advance party, which had left food caches, but farther along, storms had obliterated the trail markers and the caches. The fracturing and separating ice exposed patches of slushy holes and open water. They were forced to detour around these dangerous areas, often doubling the distance travelled to get back on track. Two men fell in, got soaked, and almost died from hypothermia. The ice was so rough that the dogs had to strain to pull the sledges and the men had to push from the rear. To protect the dogs' feet from cuts, they were outfitted with leather boots.

On February 28, both teams met to confront the first of a series of ice ridges rafted up upon each other by a storm. Storms often caused moving ice to smash up against and slide over still ice, and, according to Bartlett, the pressure of the "irresistible force meeting the immovable body" threw the ice into fantastic, mountainous formations. The first ridge stopped them in their tracks. Towering more than thirty metres high and about three miles wide, stretching as far as they could see to the west and to the east, it completely blocked their way forward. Chafe's team had been trying to get through for three days without success. They were prepared to turn back to Shipwreck Camp. Bartlett shouted and cursed at them and started to hack a path right through the first ice wall. There was no way over or around, so the remainder of the group picked up ice picks and axes to chop a passage through the massive ridges. They burrowed into the ice, creating narrow troughs and ice rubble over which it was just barely possible to haul the sledges. Progress was a few metres a day. Bartlett compared it to building an original pass through the Rocky Mountains. He regretted that he did not have a camera with him to take photographs.

While this was under way, McKinlay, Hadley, and Chafe were sent by Bartlett on a risky journey back to Shipwreck

Camp to pick up a reserve of supplies, especially oil, from the stash that had been left there. They had all the dogs harnessed to one sledge and so could make good time. The temperature dropped all the way down to -46°C, and the wind seemed to attack from all sides at once. When McKinlay's team returned a week later, the way forward had moved only five kilometres. Hadley claimed these ridges were the worst he had seen in his long years in the Arctic.

Another Arctic danger trailed the group. A polar bear looking for food came within a few feet of Hadley before he noticed the dogs growling and their hair standing on end. "If the dogs hadn't smelt [*sic*] it, I should never have known what hit me," he recalled. "The bear had blood in his eye and went for the dogs as if bent on murder." Hadley reached for his gun and "gave it to him in the head." Because of time lost at the ridges, plus the difficult travel conditions and exhaustion, Bartlett decided to head directly to Wrangel Island without any interim stopover on Herald Island or anywhere else—not that there was an "anywhere else" where it was safe to stop. But the worst was over, for now. The group was now travelling over smoother ice and making good time. Luck was with them. The weather was clear, with more daylight and temperatures around -43°C. By March 12, they had covered forty kilometres and reached land, a long sandbar extending out from the northeastern edge of Wrangel Island (Ostrov Vrangelya in Russian). The sandbar was called Icy Spit, and the name was appropriate.

Wrangel Island was (and is) a desolate chunk of land lying 142 kilometres off the coastal tundra of northeastern Siberia. At 125 kilometres wide and occupying an area of some 7,300 square kilometres between the Chukchi Sea and the East Siberian Sea, it consists of a southern coastal plain, central mountains, a northern coastal plain, and more than nine hundred small lakes. Lying well above the Arctic Circle, it has no trees, but it does have a severe polar climate, which the new arrivals began experiencing immediately.

To Bartlett's ragtag bunch, Wrangel Island was sanctuary. It was solid ground, not unstable sea ice and open water. They were so excited, they hugged each other, jumped, and shouted. Chafe recalled, "We were wild with delight. The men dug into the snow all the way down to earth so they could pick up a stone from the frozen ground." Then they set about building some igloos.

There was low-lying lichen and moss on some exposed rocks and a gravel beach strewn with the bones of whales and walruses. More driftwood was visible farther up the beach. Gathering up some of the wood scattered around, Kiruk built a fire, and by the time the first of three igloos was built, she had brewed hot tea for everyone.

The group's joy was short-lived. They had managed to bring with them enough food to last until summer. Then they would have to hunt and kill birds and seals. While the castaways had firearms and ammunition, they were not expert marksmen and would eventually run out of bullets.

The Inuit family knew how to fish, build snares, and make spears and harpoons, so they were the shipwrecked survivors' best hope to supplement a meagre diet.

A quick reconnaissance of that part of the island by Kuraluk and Kataktovik did not find any evidence of either the Anderson or Forbes-Mackay parties. Nor did they spot tracks of any wild game. The island was rarely visited, and unless someone could get to civilization and report the *Karluk*'s sinking and her survivors' location, they would be marooned here until their supplies ran out and they starved, froze to death, or went mad.

CHAPTER

8

Castaways on Wrangel Island

IN THE EARLY 1820S, Chukchi Indigenous people on the northeast Siberian coast told Baron Ferdinand Friedrich Georg Ludwig von Wrangel—a Baltic German explorer appointed commander of the Russian Kolymskaya expedition to explore their polar seas—about territory, perhaps a continent, to the north that was occasionally visible when atmospheric conditions were just right. Wrangel sailed for that remote area but, blocked by ice, failed to land. Through the years, whaling captains insisted they had seen it, but their visions were derided because the Arctic is infamous, like any desert, for its mirages (Fata Morgana phenomena), which are seen in a narrow band over sheets of ice just above the horizon.

An American polar expedition in 1879 had drifted close to Wrangel Island but did not land. However, its commander, George Washington DeLong, determined it was not a polar continent at all. His ship, the USS *Jeannette,* just like *Karluk,* had been crushed by the polar ice pack and sank after his men, too, had unloaded provisions and equipment onto the ice, some 1,280 kilometres to the northwest of Wrangel. In 1881, the steamers USS *Thomas L. Corwin* and USS *Rodgers,* looking for the lost *Jeannette* survivors, actually landed a search party on Wrangel, took possession for the US by raising a flag, and called the island New Columbia. Naturalist John Muir, who was on the *Corwin,* published the first description of Wrangel Island, calling it "this grand wilderness in its untouched freshness," this "severely solitary" land in the "topmost, frost-killed end of creation." Nothing disturbed the solitude until the next doomed expedition, Captain Bartlett and his band of castaways, made landfall there in 1914.

Bartlett's initial plan had been for them to rest briefly on Wrangel Island and then move on to the Siberian mainland. But the *Karluk* group was too large to travel en masse over even more hostile terrain. And his experience at the ice ridge had convinced him that travelling in smaller segmented teams had not been successful. It was a miracle they had made it this far. Besides, some of the men were too physically and mentally exhausted to proceed. They were so weak and frostbitten that they would never make it over the

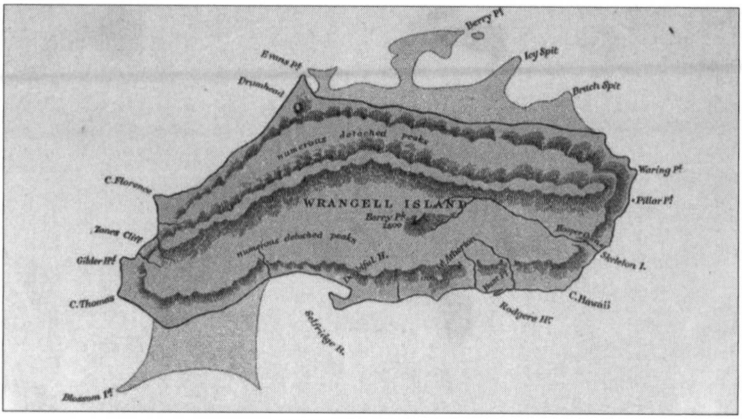

A map of Wrangel Island, showing key encampments, drawn by expedition member Bjarn Mamen.

WIKIMEDIA COMMONS, PD-CANADA; PD-US; PD-OLD-70

ever-shifting ice and open water leads to the Siberian coast, much less travel farther south to an ice-free seaport. Bartlett made a quick assessment of their situation:

> We were on land but were a long way from civilization; we need not drown but we might starve or freeze to death if we could not get help within a reasonable time. With the decline of the whaling industry there was no chance that any ship would come so far out from the mainland so that the only way to expect help to reach the party was to go after it.

Bartlett knew he was the only one with the Arctic experience and the sea-captain credentials to get help and to convince that help to return for the rest of them. It was decided, then: he would move out for the Siberian coast while the rest hunkered down in a makeshift tent camp to await rescue. The authorities in Ottawa had to be notified of the *Karluk* disaster and its marooned survivors. Six days after arriving on Wrangel Island, Bartlett and the young Alaskan Inupiat hunter Kataktovik left on a perilous 1,125-kilometre sledge journey to Siberia and then to the Bering Sea. Kataktovik was experienced in ice travel, could endure the hardships of Arctic life, and was a bachelor with no immediate family ties.

They set off March 18 in a blizzard with one sledge, food for forty-eight days, and shorter rations for seven dogs for thirty days. Speed was essential in order to get to their destination before provisions ran out and winter returned again. Besides, spring was imminent, and to wait any longer would risk dealing with even softer, looser ice.

Bartlett decided that he and Kataktovik would make time to skirt around the island's shore to the south and east in hopes of finding Anderson's or Forbes-Mackay's campsites. If they couldn't find the missing men, they would strike out across the drift ice to the mainland—not that Bartlett was confident of what he would find there. In his own words, "I knew about as much about Siberia as I knew about Mars. I felt quite certain, however, that there were natives dwelling along the coast on whom we could if necessary depend for food for our dogs and ourselves."

Bartlett had instructed the group he left behind to set up three small tent camps around the island in order to enlarge the hunting territory and improve their chances of getting game. This had the added benefit of reducing personality conflicts. By separating incompatible members, who could choose to live at an encampment where they could avoid those they disliked, he hoped to promote group harmony under trying circumstances. He told them to assemble near the south shore at Rodgers Harbour by mid-July, when there would be less ice, and look for any passing ships that might rescue them. Hopefully, Bartlett said, he would be there with a ship. He left Munro in general charge of the party in his absence and asked McKinlay to keep an inventory of supplies and try to keep the peace among the castaways. They all wrote letters home, which Bartlett took with him to post in Alaska.

Without their resolute captain, simmering resentments splintered the group into fractious cliques. These squabbles were counterproductive to survival. They were not operating as a team but as an assortment of disaffected individuals. All they could do was to wait while they struggled against starvation, snow blindness, exposure to the elements, and each other.

To make matters worse, their tent encampment was miserable, made even more so by the necessity to remain inside cold, damp, cramped quarters most of the time. Several of the men developed a mystery illness that produced extreme fatigue accompanied by swollen legs and feet. It came and went randomly. They thought it might be due to the bear meat they ate, but McKinlay noted his symptoms got worse when he ate the tinned pemmican. The cause was ultimately deduced. It was protein poisoning, a form of nephritis or kidney inflammation from eating their defective pemmican.

Traditional pemmican was the Native version of an energy bar that had sustained Arctic travellers for centuries, including Admiral Peary's expeditions. It provided basic human nutrition—quality protein, fats, and vitamins from raw sources—during travel, winter, or when wild game was scarce. Of course, the key word was "quality." As with much of the planning for the first Canadian Arctic Expedition, little attention had been paid to the condition of the supplied pemmican. Stefansson later rationalized the oversight by shifting the blame: "Our pemmican makers have failed us through supplying us with a product deficient in fat." McKinlay felt it was Stefansson who was deficient. He considered Stefansson too focused on public relations and lacking the attention to detail necessary in planning any expedition, much less one to the Arctic, as well as careless in his concern for human life. "There is not the slightest hint . . . that he accepted responsibility, as leader, for the deficiency of the pemmican, which was our staple diet, and which lead to so much suffering and loss of life."

Karluk survivors on the beach at Cape Waring, Wrangel Island, summer 1914. LIBRARY AND ARCHIVES CANADA C-071030

As winter became early spring, the castaways survived on roots, skins, and whatever birds or fish Kiruk could catch. In summer, some of the men moved up and down the coast trying to find game and better hunting grounds. They established sub-camps at Skeleton Harbour and Cape Waring along the east and southeast coasts, to the most southerly point, Rodgers Harbour, the best spot to sight ships. But the men at Rodgers Harbour fared little better than those back at Icy Spit. Bjarne Mamen developed the mystery illness and could not stand up. George Malloch, the geologist, seemed to have developed dementia. He began laughing uncontrollably and wandering out into the snow without footwear and got severe frostbite. Some of his toes had to be cut off. Bob Templeman, the cook, was exhausted trying to care for the pair.

Malloch was the first to die. Mamen became severely depressed, losing the will to live. McKinlay decided to visit their southern outpost and walked the ninety-six-kilometre distance from the initial shore camp at Icy Spit to Rodgers Point. His appearance momentarily cheered Mamen, but the latter still questioned their ultimate fate: "I do not know how this will end. Is it death for all of us?"

McKinlay thought he, Mamen, and Templeman should bury Malloch as best they could under the thin soil and rocks and mark his grave with a wooden cross. Then, after a few days' rest, they should move back to Icy Spit. But Mamen was too weak to walk, and Templeman opted to stay with him. Too feeble to bury Malloch, they covered him with a blanket and left him in the tent. McKinlay started back alone but got hopelessly lost and became snow blind. The horror of the trip affected him for the rest of his life: "It was the only time in all my experience in the ship, in the ice-pack, on the island, that I felt fear." He made it, but was in rough shape: "The soles of my boots were worn into huge holes. Where the holes were, the skin was gone, and my feet were raw and bleeding. No other trip I made compared to this one for sheer torture."

Fred Maurer and John Munro then set out for Rodgers Point to bring the two men back. As they approached the camp, they called out to Mamen and Templeman. Only Templeman came out. Tears were streaming down his face. Mamen was dead. Templeman had been sharing the tent with two dead men. It was not looking good for any of them.

In June, their diet improved when flocks of seabirds returned to nest. The birds and their eggs were an essential source of fresh food. But they were down to the last eighty rounds of ammunition for their firearms. Because their supply of seal meat was gone (at least, the best parts had been consumed), they were reduced to eating rotting flippers, blood soup, skin, or any other bits and pieces they could get into their mouths and down their throats. According to seaman Williams, there was a lot of distrust. The full sharing of collected eggs and birds among shore-camp members was questioned. Not all collected eggs made it back to camp. "Wednesday last," Williams wrote, "Breddy and Chafe really obtained 6 eggs and 5 birds instead of 2 eggs and 4 birds as they reported." It was not the first time this sort of thing had happened. Breddy had been suspected for some time of helping himself first, as well as stealing personal property from other men. Resentments continued to fester. McKinlay wrote in his diary: "On our own the misery and desperation of our situation multiplied every weakness, every quirk of personality, every flaw in character, a thousand fold." Looming over them was the knowledge that if they were not rescued by the end of August, the ice would reform and trap them there for another winter.

The third death on Wrangel Island was from a gunshot wound, probably self-inflicted but perhaps the result of foul play. On June 25, a little over a year since they had set out with great fanfare from Victoria on the *Karluk*, a loud bang split the silence of the camp. The sound came from the tent George Breddy shared with second engineer Robert Williamson. Williamson said Breddy had been cleaning his pistol and it accidently went off. The men peered into the tent and saw that Breddy was alone inside and was dead. A gun lay nearby, but seemed to be in an odd position for someone who had just shot himself in the head. It was far away from the body.

By now all the men were used to handling guns. They had access to firearms and ammunition, not just for hunting animals, but for protection from them as well. Huge polar bears could not only destroy their fragile shelters but kill the marooned survivors as well. The question now was, what had happened? Was it an accident or suicide? Nobody said anything. In Hadley's view, it was murder, and Williamson was his main suspect. Nothing could be proven, however, and Williamson would later call Hadley's suspicions "hallucinations and absolutely untrue." When Breddy's body was prepared for burial, possessions belonging to McKinlay were found among the former's personal effects. McKinlay made another observation in his diary: "Our suspicions have been raised by Williamson's strange conduct and by other circumstances that Breddy did not die by his own hand. If nothing else, his right hand was not in such a formation as would hold a revolver."

They continued to fight over the division of supplies,

tobacco, and ammunition, with the quest for food overriding all else. McKinlay described the joy of catching birds that yielded only the tiniest scraps of meat and the anguish of discovering companions stealing food from one another. Two attempts were made to go back to Shipwreck Camp for more rations or to find some of the food caches made in preparation for their February march to the island. These attempts failed because the summer ice was unstable, and they had no boat or flotation device to cross open water. Chafe made it partway but had to turn back, almost drowning when he, the sled, and the dogs all plunged into the cold water. They managed to get back up onto firmer ice but were disoriented and freezing. Chafe freed the dogs from their harness but tied one of them to his arm with a rawhide thong, hoping it would head back to camp with him in tow before he died of hypothermia. The animal had excellent homing instincts, and they made it, but Chafe was ill for days. There was no more talk of going back to Shipwreck Camp.

* * *

Despite all the hardships and talk of murder, the Canadian Red Ensign was raised at Rodgers Harbour on July 1, Dominion Day, to celebrate the forty-seventh anniversary of Confederation. The next day, Kuraluk took his family egg hunting near the cliffs. They camped out for a couple of days just to be together and away from the men at the camps. He made some toy sleds and tents for the girls, and they played with them throughout the days. Mugpi laughed and talked a lot, but Helen was more serious and worried about their situation. Occasionally, she would chase Nigeraurak with her sister, but mostly she helped her father hunt and her mother cook. Later that month, Kuraluk killed a 270-kilogram walrus, which supplied all the camps with fresh meat for weeks. August arrived and brought with it cooler temperatures that heralded the approach of another winter. Still no ship arrived. The unspoken question was, what happened to Bartlett and Kataktovik? Had they made it, or were they dead?

As time dragged by and things became ever more desperate, the men did make sure that neither the two little girls nor the cat went hungry. They became the centre of attention and were given food even if the men had to part with some of their own rations. Strange as it seemed, the cat gave them a focus other than themselves and their own desperate situations. After all, she was their good-luck charm. She had nine lives, and maybe they would too. Two young children and a small furry life gave them reason for hope: as long as Nigeraurak was alive, they would survive.

CHAPTER

9

Trek for Help

BOB BARTLETT AND KATAKTOVIK LEFT behind on Wrangel Island fifteen people, some dogs, and one cat. Their lives depended on the success of this journey. If the voyagers fell through the ice, ran out of food, got lost, froze, or simply gave up, the group's unhappy fate would be sealed.

Bartlett was not familiar with the topography of the northeastern coast of Siberia. He had never been there before and did not speak the local language, but he did know how to navigate in the North and how to survive in desperate circumstances. On March 18, Bartlett and Kataktovik began what they anticipated would be a 177-kilometre journey over the shifting, treacherous ice of the De Long Strait (Proliv Longa) from Wrangel Island to the Cape North (Mys Shmidta) coast of Siberia. This was just the first stage of their trip.

* * *

Like any travel over loose ice, it would be anything but a trip in a straight line. "From now on," Bartlett later recalled, "our journey became a never-ending series of struggles to get around or across lanes of open water—leads, as they are called—the most exasperating and treacherous of all Arctic travelling." Often the two men would split up to look for a suitable crossing, but they would never lose sight of each other. This resulted in going many extra miles just to advance a few hundred feet. At other times, they had to unhitch the dogs, throw them over a narrow lead, then place the sledge over the opening and use it as a bridge to get across—all the while hoping the dogs would not run off or that the sledge, with them on top of it, would not drop into the cold water. Sometimes the lead was too wide for this technique, and the pair would have to look for a floating ice cake or a piece of ice jutting out from the floe that they would break off and use as a raft to float themselves, the dogs, and the sledge across, using their snowshoes as paddles. Having crossed one lead, they were faced with an ongoing series of dark, gaping leads as they crossed the De Long Strait between Wrangel Island and Siberia.

The sea ice they had to cross cracked and shifted constantly under their weight. Every night, after an exhausting day of zigzag travel, they built their sleeping igloo, which usually took about forty-five minutes, on solid ice. Then they had some biscuit, pemmican, and hot tea made with melted snow and nodded off immediately. One night, they were rudely awakened around 2:00 AM when the ice beneath them started to sag and they were sinking into a slushy black hole. They scrambled out just in time to grab the dogs and watch as their stove, blankets, and dry clothing dropped out of sight. At least they still had the sledge, with most of their supplies. They were in constant pain from frostbite and snow blindness (a painful eye condition, also known as "photokeratitis," caused by unprotected exposure to ultraviolet light reflected from ice and snow). Also, Bartlett did not feel well after eating some pemmican. As they moved forward, closer and closer to the safety of land, Kataktovik became increasingly agitated, and Bartlett demanded to know what was wrong. He explained that the Siberian Inuit were the mortal enemies of his Alaskan Inuit tribe, and he believed they would kill him on sight. Bartlett tried to reassure him that nothing bad would happen, but Kataktovik did not believe one man could do much against so many.

On April 4, they set foot on solid ground again, just west of Cape North. They saw igloos in the far distance. Bartlett rechecked the charts he had brought with him from the *Karluk* just to confirm that this really was the mainland and not just another island. He then consulted his reference text, *American Coast Pilot*, which had the following reassuring words: "The northeast coast of Siberia has been only slightly examined, and the charts must be taken as sketches and only approximately accurate."

As they approached the igloos, they could see they were low circular structures made of bent saplings under snow-covered stretched walrus skins. They were immediately approached and surrounded by a party of Siberian Inuit, who Bartlett described as "Chukches" [Chukchis]. Kataktovik was ready to go down fighting, but they appeared friendly. Using hand gestures, the Inuit led Bartlett and Kataktovik to a dwelling and invited them inside, where they were given food. Their hosts unhitched the dogs, fed them, and brought the sled inside out of the elements. Bartlett found the lodging "smelled worse than any Greenland igloo I have ever been in, which is saying a good deal." Kataktovik was immensely relieved his life did not appear to be threatened. In addition to feeding them reindeer meat washed down with black Russian tea, the residents, who numbered about a dozen, provided warm bedding, hung their clothes up to dry, and helped mend their parkas and dog harnesses. According to Bartlett, "Never have I been entertained in a finer spirit of true hospitality and never have I been more thankful for the cordiality of my welcome."

* * *

They had travelled over 322 kilometres in seventeen days and could have stayed to recuperate, but Bartlett, worried about the food supplies back on Wrangel Island, insisted on pushing forward after only two nights' rest. Pulling out his charts, he pointed out where they had been and where they wanted to go. Diagrams and maps were better communications devices than words, and their hosts pointed out the route they would take. As parting gifts, he left their hosts with some of the Indian pressed-tea tablets salvaged from the *Karluk* and distributed the brightly coloured tins to the children. He also left other small articles that were useful for barter including a couple of wristwatches, some razors, a cake of soap, sewing needles, matches, and a pocket knife. Money, of which he had a little, mostly borrowed from Hadley, was not of much interest.

Bartlett and Kataktovik were tired, but their sled dogs were exhausted. Unfortunately, the coastal Natives did not have many dogs and could spare only two. So other than these two, the pair continued with their own dogs.

The Bering Strait was still 804 kilometres away. Bartlett estimated this would take about three weeks, even using the light of the midnight sun and sledding until 3:00 AM. As they moved south, the two men encountered more small Inuit settlements whose residents willingly shared what food and shelter they had with the strange voyagers.

It was lucky they did so. The temperature dropped to -50°C, and Bartlett had never been so cold in his life, not even near the North Pole. Gale-force winds made it difficult to stand up, much less move forward easily. The name *Siberia* aptly translates to "Sleeping Country": the only things moving on the snow-covered landscape were the two men, their exhausted dogs, and their sled. On April 24, they reached Emma Town (a village that no longer exists, located a few miles southwest of East Cape, on the Chukchi Peninsula, and the Siberian port closest to Alaska). "The second stage of our journey from Wrangel Island was over," Bartlett wrote in his logbook. "We had been thirty-seven days on the march and . . . had actually travelled about seven hundred miles, all but the last part of the way on foot. There now remained the question of transportation to Alaska, and the sooner I was able to arrange for that the better."

At Emma Town, Bartlett discussed transport to Alaska with local residents. There were four options, none of them ideal. He could cross the Bering Strait on sea ice by island-hopping via a circuitous route to the two Diomede Islands, then to Cape Prince of Wales and on to Nome, but it was too late in the season to do that safely. Option two was to wait until sometime in June, when the summer trading ships started calling in at East Cape (now known as Cape Dezhnev), and try to hitch a ride back with one of them. Option three was to wait until the first week of June, when a Mr. Thompson, who owned the local trading store at Emma Harbor, would be sailing his schooner directly to Nome and could take the captain with him. Emma Harbor (now

Komsomolskaya Bay) is a large, sheltered bay on the eastern shore of Providence Bay, a fjord on the Chukchi Peninsula of northeastern Siberia.

The most pressing need was to send that telegram to Ottawa as soon as possible, telling officials about the *Karluk* disaster and the Wrangel survivors waiting to be rescued. Bartlett chose a fourth option—to travel to the wireless station at Anadyr, the most easterly town in Russia. Inuit guides would take him there, and Kataktovik would remain at East Cape. Kataktovik wanted to return to Point Hope, Alaska, so Bartlett gave him provisions to last until he could get on a ship going there in June. With their course of action decided, Bartlett went to bed for a good night's sleep. He awoke in pain with swollen legs and feet, and now his throat as well, all of which he attributed to his relentless march of the past months. No matter the reason, he could not move. Then he developed an acute case of tonsillitis. He and Kataktovik had lost over fourteen kilograms each, and both were too ill to carry on. Their quest was over. There would be no telegram—not yet, at any rate.

* * *

Luck then intervened in the person of Baron Kleist, the Russian supervisor of northeastern Siberia and Kamchatka. Kleist was based in Emma Town and took an interest in their mission. His party was leaving on May 10 for Emma Harbor, and he offered to take Bartlett with him on his sledge. It was a week-long trip, but once there, Bartlett could look for an early ship directly to Alaska. It was a better option than trying to make it to Anadyr in his current condition. Bartlett and Kataktovik parted company. Bartlett gave him the rifle he had brought from the *Karluk*. It was an emotional goodbye because Bartlett knew what a steadfast companion Kataktovik had been, standing by the captain when others would have abandoned their enterprise. The wages due him would be paid when Bartlett got back to Nome. Baron Kleist was anxious to get under way before a thaw would break up the ice on the rivers and slow his journey. The distance from East Cape to Emma Harbor was 306 kilometres along a foggy, rainy coastal route. The dogs would have to be fed, but this late in the season, Inuit along the way would have little meat to spare, so they had to bring a supply. Bartlett left his own exhausted team at East Cape.

As they moved south through what Bartlett described as "wild country," the fog became even denser, and they had to navigate by compass because visibility was so poor that they could not see beyond the baron's lead dog. They were soaked through, and when they stopped to rest at a Native dwelling, Bartlett took the opportunity to dry out his clothes. He knew that if you became sick or injured in the Arctic, it could be a death sentence, and he had an important mission to complete.

They frequently sledged late into the night or started

before dawn, but on one occasion they overnighted at a settlement that had a herd of reindeer, and they feasted on cooked reindeer meat.

Bartlett was recovering but still rode on a sledge. (It was standard practice for a musher to stand at the rear of the sled and push with one foot while keeping the other on a runner, or push from the rear himself if the dogs were tired, the snow was deep or soggy, and the sledding tough for the animals.) "We averaged four or five miles an hour," he wrote. "Our dog-drivers were skilful and knew what they were about."

The schooner for Nome was not scheduled to leave until early June, but at one stop, a resident told them about a whaling ship at Indian Point under the command of a man named C.D. Pedersen. Bartlett surmised this was the same man he had replaced as captain of the *Karluk*, and, in the small community of ships' masters, the skippers were acquainted with each other. Bartlett was delighted and hoped he could persuade Pedersen to take him to Alaska.

Very early on May 16, Bartlett and the baron had almost made it to their destination. All that remained was to cross the cliffs that protected the harbour. It was a gruelling climb to the top, then a frantic descent down the other side as dogs and men careened out of control. For the short time he spent at the peak, Bartlett got a glimpse of Emma Harbor and could "see open water out into Providence Bay. The land was white with snow and . . . the open water beyond seemed

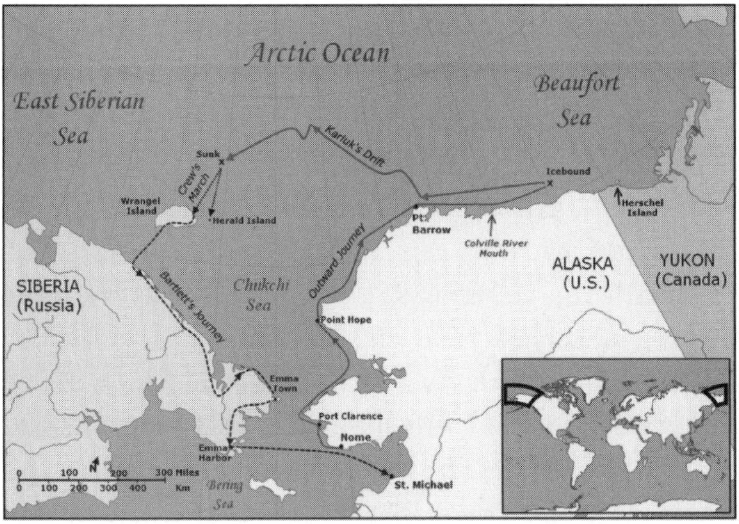

Map of the voyage of the *Karluk* and Bartlett's journey on foot to rescue survivors. NORMAN EINSTEIN, WIKIMEDIA COMMONS

as black as coal-tar." The trip had taken six days, and Bartlett noted in his logbook, "Two months had gone by since I had parted from the men on Icy Spit, Wrangel Island. If all went well I should be back for them in two months more."

At 7:00 AM on May 16, they arrived at the baron's residence. Bartlett was impressed:

> It was a fine house well built of heavy timbers, the materials having been brought from Vladivostok five years before. It cost about fifteen thousand dollars and was warm and comfortable. The baron had an excellent chef and we enjoyed a substantial breakfast. Then the baron's own physician,

> Doctor Golovkoff, who had been with him through the Russo-Japanese War, looked after my legs and throat. He took me under his especial care during my stay and had me in pretty good condition by the time I left.

Bartlett inquired about Captain Pedersen. He learned the two men had even more in common than their *Karluk* association. In autumn 1913, when the *Karluk* had been drifting in ice, Pedersen's ship the *Elvira* was crushed by ice and sank off Alaska's north coast. He had travelled overland on foot to Fairbanks and caught a ship back to San Francisco, where he was assigned to the whaling and trading ship SS *Herman*. Bartlett dispatched a number of Chukchis to locations where Pedersen might dock, with notes asking if he could get a free lift back to Alaska. He need not have bothered. Pedersen had already heard of Bartlett's trek through the Native grapevine and from a trading-store owner. On May 21, the *Herman* steamed into Emma Harbor. Bartlett's ride had arrived.

CHAPTER

10

From Russia to Alaska

PEDERSEN GRACIOUSLY WELCOMED BARTLETT ON board and offered to transport him back to Alaska. Pedersen had a minority interest of 20 percent in the profit or loss from the *Herman*'s whaling and trading business. Permission from the other owners for this unscheduled detour still meant Pedersen and his crew would have their pay delayed until they could resume servicing their commercial contacts. After thanking Baron Kleist for his generosity, Bartlett immediately boarded the *Herman* and sailed for Nome through loose ice floating on the surface of the Bering Sea. Bartlett, still not fully recovered from his illness, took the time on the 386-kilometre trip to finish recuperating. Pedersen provided him with some North

American clothing to replace the furs he had been wearing for the past months.

When they arrived on May 24, Nome was ice-locked, and no ship could get through. They were held nineteen kilometres offshore. For three days, they waited outside the icefield. If they entered and got stuck, they could be trapped indefinitely until the ice pack broke up. So near but yet so far: Bartlett was beyond frustrated.

On May 27, Pedersen diverted south to St. Michael, founded in 1833 as a Russian-American trading post for commerce with the Yupik people. After the fog lifted around 6:00 PM, they were able to enter the harbour, launch a small boat to the edge of shore ice, and walk onto American territory. Bartlett went directly to the wireless station to send a telegram to Ottawa reporting that he, and some passengers on Wrangel Island, were alive, but that the *Karluk* was no more. It was 8:00 PM, and the station was closed. No messages would be going out that evening. Ever resourceful, Bartlett appealed to the local US marshal, who, in another convenient coincidence, had served with Admiral Peary and with whom Bartlett had talked the previous summer, when the *Karluk* was Arctic-bound. They talked again at the local hotel about the *Karluk*, the survivors' predicament, the captain's trek for help, and what ships were in the area.

The next morning, the station was open. But the operator would not send an urgent message unless payment was made in full up front. Bartlett, who had very little money with him, cooled his temper and again appealed to his friend, the US marshal. The marshal directed the operator to send the dispatch as part of his regular duties, or he would no longer have any regular duties. It began:

> St. Michael's [sic], Alaska,
> May 29, 1914.
> Naval Service, Ottawa, Canada
>
> Karluk ice pressure sank January 11, sixty miles north Herald Island. January twenty-first sent first and second mate two sailors with supporting party three months provisions Wrangell [*sic*] Island. February fifth Mackay, Murray, Beuchat, Sailor Morris left us using man power pull sledge. March twelfth landed Munro, Williamson, Malloch, McKinlay, Mamen, Hadley, Chafe, Templeman, Maurer, Breddy, Williams, Eskimo family Wrangell eighty-six days' supplies each man. March eighteenth I left island [with] Eskimo landed Siberia fifty miles west Cape North. May twenty-first Captain Pederson Whaler *Herman* called for me Emma Harbor.

The telegram ended with:

> Soundings meteorological observations dredging kept up continually. Successful. Twelve hundred fathoms animal life found bottom. Need funds pay bills contracted Siberia and here. Wire Northern Commercial Company, San Francisco, five hundred dollars. Instruct them forward by wire St. Michael's.
>
> Bartlett, Captain, C.G.S.

To the Naval Service officials in Ottawa, who had believed the *Karluk* and all her company were lost, this was a dispatch out of the blue. The bureaucrats were vastly relieved. They asked about rescue plans. Bartlett suggested contacting the Russian government, which had powerful icebreakers in the Chukchi Sea, and the Americans, who had the Revenue Cutter Service (later Coast Guard) SS *Bear* in the Bering Sea. Any and all assistance was welcome—indeed, it was required, and quickly. Ships must be ready to go as soon as navigation opened up because, as they had found with the *Karluk*, the period of open water was brief and could be cut short at any moment. Bartlett followed up with Ottawa, giving specific instructions so there would be no misunderstanding:

St. Michael's [*sic*], Alaska,
May 30, 1914.

Hon. G.J. Desbarats,
Naval Service, Ottawa, Canada.

Russian ice-breakers *Taimir* and *Vaigatch* soon make annual exploring trip north coast Siberia. Strongly advise you try arrange Russian Government these vessels relieve men. Vessels wintered Vladivostock [*sic*] but may have already left for north. Failing this arrangement another Russian ice-breaker *Nadjeshny* lying idle Vladivostock might be obtained. Another chance United States Revenue Cutter *Bear* now in Bering Sea. Possible arrangements United States Government. If *Bea*r goes, should seek convoy Russian ice-breakers. No

> vessels these waters. My opinion July or early August before ice breaks up around Wrangell [*sic*] though seasons differ. Plenty bird other animal life island good Eskimo hunter should not suffer food. I want go relief ships. Russian ships have wireless can get in touch with them *if* already at sea.
>
> Bartlett, Captain.

Although Bartlett was desperate to arrange the rescue of the castaways he knew he had left on Wrangel Island, he still had hope, however faint, that Anderson's party and Forbes-Mackay's party had by now made it to land, either on Wrangel Island or on the Arctic mainland. The primary objective was to get back to Wrangel, but he had not forgotten about the others.

* * *

When the Canadian government released news that the captain of the *Karluk* and its passengers, long presumed dead, were alive, Bartlett was an immediate hero. He received many joyful messages from his family in Newfoundland and from friends in Boston and along the seacoast. They all knew he would make it, they said, just not that it would take so long. Congratulatory telegrams poured in from around the world, and reporters called up to ask for interviews. The advertising department of an American magazine asked to run a photo of him smoking his pipe to accompany one of their tobacco ads: "Please wire our expense permission to use your picture smoking pipe for tobacco advertisement. What brand do you smoke?"

Bartlett could not have cared less; his only concern was to rescue his castaways. He was anxious to return to Wrangel Island, even though ice was still an impediment to ocean travel. He reiterated that the best time to make a try would be in July, when the ice was thinner. Meanwhile, Bartlett travelled to Nome, now free of heavy ice, where he became preoccupied with finding a ship to take him north. He sent word out to every captain of every ship leaving for northern waters, asking them to scout out Wrangel Island if they were in the area. If he could not help the castaways himself, maybe somebody else could. Later, when Pedersen stopped in Nome, Bartlett wired his ship's owners for additional permission to go north with the *Herman* and pick up the survivors on Wrangel Island. They declined, saying he should go about his business and let the *Bear* go to the rescue.

In a situation eerily similar to that of the *Karluk* and the Canadian Arctic Expedition, the *Bear*, a Scotland-built sealer that had operated off Newfoundland, had been one of the ships instrumental in rescuing survivors of the Greely Expedition (also known as the Lady Franklin Bay Expedition) on the other side of the North American continent in 1884. Dispatched as part of the United States's participation in the first International Polar Year (1882–1883), the Greely Expedition consisted of twenty-five scientists and crew sent to Ellesmere Island, off the northwest coast of Greenland. They were commanded by Adolphus W. Greely, a lieutenant in the Army Signal Corps, the branch responsible for weather stations and meteorological observations.

One of the goals of the Greely Expedition was to establish an Arctic research station to serve as a link in a chain of internationally built geophysical observation stations around the Arctic Circle. Unfortunately, the ship sent to resupply them in the summer of 1882 was forced to turn back because of ice, and the men were left without supplies. Food ran low, and some of the group began to sicken and die. Their spare rations were supplemented with tiny native shrimps, rock moss, and lichen, but accusations of theft from the dwindling food supply flared. A second relief ship, sent in 1883, was crushed in the ice. Expedition members spent a third, wretched winter camped at Cape Sabine in what is now Nunavut. Supplies ran out, hunting failed, men died of starvation. At last, in the summer of 1884, the six survivors were brought home by a military rescue mission that included the *Bear.*

The excitement of the survivors' return soon turned into a national scandal as rumours of cannibalism were supported by grisly evidence. In 1885, the *Bear* was transferred to the Treasury Department for use in Alaskan waters and the Arctic Ocean. And there she worked, now ready to rescue Bob Bartlett's castaways on Wrangel Island.

* * *

When the Americans placed the *Bear* at Bartlett's disposal to rescue his stranded party, he was ecstatic. He called her "a crack sealer for the period that had made many successful voyages." She was a three-masted, dual steam-powered and sailing ship, her keel made from greenheart, a dense yet flexible wood from South America. If any ship could navigate through the impenetrable ice surrounding Wrangel Island, this was it. Her current master, Captain Cochran, was known to Bartlett by reputation only. That reputation was of a skilled mariner who was "not afraid to put her into the ice." Bartlett felt it was appropriate "for *Bear* to rescue the *Karluk* survivors as she had rescued the Greely party thirty years before, on the other side of the continent." Until departure, Bartlett busied himself catching up on current events: "The boys at the wireless station were kind enough to give me the back files to read, so that I could get an idea of what had been happening in the world news."

On July 13, the *Bear* left Nome with Bartlett on board. He shared Cochran's cabin, spending most of his time in the chart room checking currents and ice conditions. As the *Bear* steamed along the Alaskan coast, she also served as public transit, dropping off and picking up teachers and preachers moving to new assignments, delivering mail and medical supplies, as well as conveying judges who conducted travelling courts.

Bartlett just wanted to get to Wrangel Island, but

already they were running into heavy, closely packed sea ice. At Port Hope, he was overjoyed to meet up again with Kataktovik, who had hitched a ride back from East Cape on a later ship. Kataktovik looked fully recovered from their arduous trek and announced he was engaged to be married. Bartlett congratulated him, paid him his owed wages, and presented him with a voucher from the Canadian government for a set of new clothes. This clothing allowance was given to every survivor of the *Karluk*'s sinking to replace some of their losses when the ship went down.

* * *

A Canadian schooner called the *King and Winge*, under Captain Olaf Swenson, had accompanied the *Bear* to Point Barrow. She was used to hunt walrus and as a trading vessel that carried provisions for the North West Mounted Police post at Herschel Island. Bartlett checked her over as the ice-fields thickened. She was light but powered for a top speed of only eleven knots (twenty kilometres an hour) and definitely not an icebreaker. No extra sheathing or stem plates had been added to her hull for protection. However, she was amazingly successful at combatting the ice, with her narrow, pointy bow breaking through every time. Bartlett's assessment was that she was "just in the right ballast for bucking the ice; besides being small, she was short for her beam and was quick to answer the helm." On August 23, the *Bear* left Point Barrow on a northwest heading for Wrangel Island. Through all the preceding months, Bartlett had never doubted his marooned shipmates would be rescued. Now he was steaming across the Arctic Ocean, and the only thing that could slow him down, but not stop him, was the weather. Thick fog and thick ice were always impediments, but, as he wrote in his logbook, "my feeling of relief at being at last on the way to the goal of all my thought and effort may be imagined." He was glad he was on the *Bear* and relished seeing her "charging and recharging, twisting and turning; being heavy in the water she was able, with her great momentum, to smash off points and corners of the ice and make her way through it."

The *Bear* soon became engulfed in a fog bank so thick that for days it was impossible to see what lay ahead. Once or twice, it cleared enough for Bartlett to see some birds in the distance, which suggested land. They had been pushing through heavy, densely packed ice interspersed with small sections of loose ice, but it was taking a toll on the engines and their fuel reserves. Bartlett estimated they were about thirty-two kilometres from Wrangel Island. Then came the devastating news: they would have to return to Nome to restock coal for the engines and then come back and try again. If they ran out of engine power where they were, they would be helpless in the currents and pack ice. What had happened to the *Karluk* would then happen to the *Bear*. So close to completing the rescue, they turned around. They were, said Bartlett, "days to try a man's soul. In fact, until the final rescue of the men, I spent such a wretched time as I had never had in my life."

In Nome came more bad news. He learned the Russian icebreakers had approached to within sixteen kilometres of Wrangel on August 4, but, receiving news that war had been declared, were ordered to turn back south immediately to Anadyr and join the war effort. Getting his people off Wrangel Island was proving more difficult for Captain Bob Bartlett than leading them there in the first place.

While waiting for the *Bear* to take on more coal, Bartlett had another stroke of luck when he met Captain Swenson of the *King and Winge* at a tavern popular with sailors. Swenson had returned to Nome after making a delivery to Herschel Island and was now chartered for a trading and walrus-hunting trip to the Siberian coast. Was it possible, Bartlett asked Swenson, to swing by Wrangel Island when he was in the area and check for his stranded *Karluk* party? Swenson promised to do so. Still, Bartlett could not relax. He sent a telegram to Ottawa telling government authorities what ships were involved in the search and asking for more resources. On September 4, the refuelled *Bear* left Nome with Bartlett standing on deck—his station for the next three days—looking into the distance. The water was smooth as glass, and he knew that meant there was ice up ahead. Then it came, stretching as far as the eye could see, white and solid. The *Bear* moved in and tackled it head on. By the early afternoon of September 8, they had travelled more than 80 kilometres and were about 120 kilometres from their target.

CHAPTER

11

The Rescue

IF A SHIP DID NOT COME, Kuraluk wanted the castaways on Wrangel Island to consolidate their scattered tent camps to the west side of the north coast while they built a winter cabin there near the bank of a river. At that location, he had discovered a great deal of driftwood, more than enough to construct a warmer dwelling for the dark, cold months. There were fish in the river and probably walrus nearby. Hadley also thought it was a good idea—and he had noticed a flock of geese there, too. The others agreed. If they were not rescued and had to spend another winter on Wrangel Island, this was their best option. They would begin building by mid-September.

* * *

Early on their third day at sea, September 7, 1914, the crew of the *King and Winge* saw the central mountains of Wrangel Island rolling up out of the pre-dawn ice and mist. The ice pack offshore was piled in massive pressure ridges, some over ninety metres high—higher than the ship's mast. Captain Swenson was doing what he had promised to do, look for the *Karluk*'s survivors. He had delayed his Siberian mission and had purchased an umiak, an open boat made of waterproofed skins stretched over a wood or bone frame that the Inuit used to transport people and goods. Through the icefield, Swenson and his crew now carefully surveyed the shore coming up to Rodgers Harbour, looking for signs of human life.

Then they saw it: a tattered tent flapping in the wind. When it was new, it probably would have sheltered four people; now it did not appear to have any inhabitants. There were no dogs, no sleds, and no signs of life. A wooden cross was sticking out of the ground, and a flagpole, but certainly not the twenty-three people they had hoped would be awaiting rescue. The captain blew the ship's whistle again and again. Between blasts, everyone on board watched and waited. Nothing. Then the tent flap opened, and a thin, crouched figure moved slowly forward. He didn't wave his arms or shout. He just stood up straight and stared while passing his hand in front of his eyes.

Swenson dropped anchor, launched the umiak, and sent a shore party over to identify this living skeleton. It was chief engineer John Munro. In a weak voice, Munro explained that the cross was for Malloch and Mamen, who had both died there and been buried beneath a pile of stones. Munro told them other survivors were at a summer camp near Cape Waring and they were still alive. Maurer and Templeman, who were also present but had hung back, confirmed Munro's report and asked when they could leave. Having few personal items to collect, they boarded immediately, and the *King and Winge* set sail up the coast to find the others. It all happened so fast that their deliverance seemed a dream to the three crew members.

* * *

Early on the morning of September 7, McKinlay, Hadley, Chafe, Williams, Williamson, and the Inuit family began sorting their meagre supplies in preparation for the move to the winter encampment. Kuraluk went searching for material to make a spear point, while Hadley and McKinlay remained inside their tent, making traps and trying to fix the stove. Then they heard Kuraluk's excited yelling—something about an umiak. They went outside to investigate. Could it be a ship? Kuraluk had spotted the mast of the *King and Winge* offshore, and Hadley fired his pistol into the air to attract their attention. But it looked like the schooner was sailing away. Then they watched as the sails came down and a party of rescuers disembarked and moved over the ice to the beach. The survivors did not rush forward to greet them; too dazed to speak, they just stood and looked. The rescuers gathered around the long-lost *Karluk* survivors, asking questions: Who were they? Were there any others? Were they ill? Did they want food?

A cinematographer had joined the *King and Winge* in Nome, hoping to record a one-of-a-kind story. Now, he followed the shuffling, grimy men with matted hair and beards around as they began gathering up the few possessions they still had. Nigeraurak, awakened from her morning nap by all the commotion, was bundled onto the ship as well. She had grown from the scrawny kitten, "recruited" at the Esquimalt Naval Yard over a year ago, into a sleek cat with a shiny coat.

They left the flimsy tents standing and tied notes to the poles to inform any other rescuers who might show up that the castaways had been found. Weak and emaciated as they were, all of them believed they could easily walk the three miles over the ice to where the ship was anchored, but the cameraman insisted each be supported by two crew members. "It probably made a better picture," Hadley recalled with a cynical smile.

Of the six scientists left on the *Karluk* after the departure of Stefansson, McKinlay was the sole survivor. Now, his heart was racing. They were saved! Captain Bartlett had gotten through. Eight months after the loss of the *Karluk*, they were finally on their way home.

* * *

The ship headed for nearby Herald Island to look for signs of the other two parties that had set out from the *Karluk*. It was no use. The ice would not allow them to land or even get close to shore. Crew members scanned the shore through binoculars but could see nothing. Following the unsuccessful attempt to break through the ice around Herald, the *King and Winge* turned south on September 8 for the return journey to Nome. On board, all the survivors were told the latest news about the war that was consuming Europe. The survivors found it difficult to grasp how so many people could be killing each other when their main objective over the months since the *Karluk* sank had been to stay alive.

Their greatest luxuries on the return trip were warm baths, shaves, and clean clothes. They were starting to feel normal again, but they looked as if they had aged ten years in the one-year span since the *Karluk* had left Victoria. Assembling in the galley for cup after cup of hot coffee and cigarettes, they sat around a table and gorged on toast with real butter, eggs, cereal, and sweetened condensed milk—anything but seal meat! They could hardly taste the food because their deprivations had so affected their sense of taste, so it was impossible to appreciate the flavours of their favourite meals. But they were so happy to be finally rescued that they did not care. They remembered the texture and the aroma, and savoured every mouthful. "God bless the 7th of September!" McKinlay wrote in his diary. "God bless the *King & Winge*, her skipper & her crew!!!"

Rescued survivors of the *Karluk* on board the schooner *King and Winge*. Left to right: John Munro (at rear), Robert Templeman, Robert Williamson, John Hadley, Captain Robert Bartlett, Kiruk, Mugpi, Helen, William McKinlay, Kuraluk (seated in front), Ernest Chafe, Hugh Williams, Fred Maurer. LIBRARY AND ARCHIVES CANADA PA-105130

Heading north from Nome with a full load of coal, the *Bear*, with Bartlett on board, was 121 kilometres from Wrangel Island on September 8 when she met the schooner *King and Winge*, which was headed south. There were only two possible explanations for her position, Bartlett thought: either she'd had a mechanical problem, or she had been to Wrangel Island. Bartlett could hardly believe she had made it so late in the season, with so much ice around. He grabbed binoculars and scanned the figures on deck. They looked familiar, but they were thinner and more haggard than the people he remembered. Then he recognized Munro, McKinlay, Chafe, and the Inuit family, with Helen holding the cat. Since March, he had thought so many times that he would never see any of them again.

The group on the deck of the *King and Winge* started shouting and waving as they recognized their rumpled captain. The two vessels hove to, and, taking a small boat alongside, Bartlett immediately asked if everyone was on board. They all rushed forward to shake his hand and tell their stories. "Are you all here?" Bartlett asked again. He was told there were six others below deck, but three of the people he had guided to Wrangel Island, Malloch, Mamen, and Breddy, had died. Bartlett wrote, "It was an especially sad and bitter blow to learn that three of the men whom I had seen arrive at Wrangell [*sic*] Island had thus reached safety only to die."

Bartlett now had to acknowledge there was no hope that either Dr. Forbes-Mackay's party or First Officer Anderson's party had survived. It was a melancholy moment during the joyful reunion. Of the twenty-five people who had escaped the *Karluk* sinking, eleven had died—eight trying to travel over treacherous ice, two of disease, and one by gunshot. Still, the scientists and crew, with no survival training and no Arctic experience, had persevered while relying on their captain to come through for them. Without the skill and caring of the Inuit family, the toll would have been much higher.

Later, Bartlett had all the survivors transferred over to the *Bear*. They did not want to leave the ship that had found and saved them, but the *King and Winge* had a charter contract to Siberia, and the *Bear* was returning to Nome and had a doctor on board. It took less than an hour to transfer over the entire party and their few possessions. McKinlay had quickly cleared out his tent on Wrangel Island, and now all that remained on his bunk aboard the *Bear* were the few personal items that had survived shipwreck, ice, theft, and hardship. He had abandoned his old clothing and furs, and the others did likewise. They wanted to leave all the bad memories behind.

Bartlett still did not want to accept the fate of his first officer's party and the doctor's. He asked Captain Cochran of the *Bear* to steam north to Herald Island for one last search. With a heavy heart, Bartlett described this final, fruitless attempt:

> At eight o'clock the next morning, September 9, we were twelve miles from Herald Island. The ice kept us from getting any nearer, and after we had done what we could to find a way through, and seeing no sign of human life, we headed back to Nome . . . It was very hard for me to give them up, men with whom I had spent so many months, men with the future still before them.

Bartlett had packed clothing and supplies on board the *Bear* for his shipwrecked survivors. Their first taste of real luxury was to find their bunks had been made up with quality linens, something they had not enjoyed for over a year. On the return trip, the doctor examined and questioned each one. He treated the effects of frostbite, infected lacerations, immunodeficiency, malnutrition, and confirmed that their mystery disease was indeed nephritis, an inflammation of the kidneys caused by too much dietary protein and fat. And yes, the pemmican was the culprit. When they still had a supply of biscuits from the ship, the carbohydrate balanced the protein and they were fine. The fresh meat was good, too, but there had not been enough of it. The pemmican, which was supposed to have kept them alive, had killed Malloch and Mamen and made the others ill. It had also affected Bartlett and Kataktovik on their Siberian trek. They were lucky it had not killed all of them.

* * *

Bartlett did not press the survivors about the hardships on Wrangel Island, believing the details would come out when they were ready to speak about their harrowing experiences. He learned that they had only forty rounds of ammunition remaining at Cape Waring with which to hunt for food during the coming winter. In travelling over the ice to try to retrieve a cache of food, seaman Williams had frozen his big toe so badly that there was nothing left to do but amputate to save the foot and prevent further complications. Bartlett recounted what he was told:

> Many people would have preferred to risk one danger at a time, rather than be operated on with the means at hand. Second engineer Williamson was the surgeon; he had shown his natural deftness . . . by his care of Mamen's dislocated knee-cap at Shipwreck Camp. His instruments consisted of a pocket-knife and a pair of tin-shears. Perhaps no more painful and primitive operation was ever performed in the Arctic, though the whaling captains have frequently had to exercise a rough and ready surgery . . . Williamson did his work well, and his patient did his part with rare grit, so that the result was a success.

They reached Nome on September 13 and were welcomed by throngs of well-wishers, reporters, photographers, seamen, and citizens—all of whom were curious to see the *Karluk* survivors and its captain who had never given up. Their reception was reminiscent of their joyful departure from Victoria at the start of the first Canadian Arctic Expedition. Not fully recovered and still frail with weakened immune systems, they did not disembark and walk among the crowd but stayed on deck. To walk in shoes again, after so many months of wearing skin-boots, would be painful for a while. Also, Bartlett reasoned, "It would be the irony of fate for them to survive six months of semi-starvation and then to fall victim to some ailment of the civilization to which they had so longed to return."

Before doing anything else, the survivors contacted friends and family, who were shocked and elated at the news they were alive. When search parties had turned up nothing, all had presumed the men had been lost at sea. "I do not know how or where to begin; indeed I know nothing just now," began William Laird McKinlay's letter home to his family. "Just think of it all of you—I am alive. And more than alive—I am living. None of you know what life is, nor will you ever know until you come as near losing it as we were. Think of it again; I am alive, and not lying on the pitiless Arctic floes or buried beneath the unfriendly soil of Wrangel Island."

Only after the survivors had reconnected with their loved ones did Bartlett allow the editor of the local daily newspaper and a photographer access to them. Bartlett appointed McKinlay as spokesman. "We were questioned," wrote McKinlay. "We were photographed a thousand and one times, we were offered the freedom of the town, we were invited to this, that, and the other thing; in short, we were made lions of." But access was not provided to Burt McConnell, Stefansson's personal secretary, who had abandoned the *Karluk* along with the five-man pseudo-hunting party near Point Barrow the previous September. No longer employed by the expedition, he had shown up as a freelance writer and expected to conduct interviews with the survivors. He would then telegraph rescue stories to the newspapers with which Stefansson had contracts. Bartlett was a step ahead: he had sent the story out the night before. McConnell was furious, and Bartlett was pleased.

They left Nome, homeward bound, on September 19, but the *Bear* was still a working ship in spite of her acclaimed passengers and had a number of stops to make along the way. On the afternoon of October 14, with the long homeward pennant flying, they pulled away from the pier at Unalaska in the Aleutian Islands. Bartlett recalled:

> We steamed south on the last leg of the long journey we had travelled since that June day the year before when we had first left for the north. The voyage south was uneventful and on October 24, 1914, the *Bear* landed us once more at the navy yard at Esquimalt. The next day, under the instructions of the Canadian Government, I paid off the men; soon they had started for their homes, while I left for Ottawa to make my final report of the last voyage of the *Karluk*.

CHAPTER

12

The Aftermath

THE FOURTEEN SURVIVORS OF THE sunken *Karluk* came back as heroes for surviving in the frozen North. They had been given up for dead, and now they were alive. As Europe settled in for a protracted war, the global press focused on the courageous rescue saga that had gotten the castaways off Wrangel Island. When the story about the man who had turned disaster into victory broke, the *New York Times* devoted a full-page spread to it, equivalent to the coverage of the first battles of the First World War.

The Southern Party of the CAE had successfully carried out their geographical and ethnological work and had returned home only when they were called up for active military service at the end of 1915. For Stefansson, as expedition leader, to leave the flagship of the Northern Party as he did was certainly inappropriate but not criminal. Nor did he look back after the loss of the *Karluk*: he arranged for more ships and supplies and hired more men so that his Northern Party of the CAE could extend its work in the Western Arctic until 1918, discovering the last unmapped islands of northern Canada. But raising flags and erecting plaques are meaningless gestures if not accompanied by effective occupation or administration. Today, extended continental shelf claims to polar waters and seabed are asserted by Canada, Denmark, Norway, Russia, and the US. The value of Arctic territory is not so much in shipping as in possible oil and gas reserves. During the Cold War years, Canada relocated Inuit families in the Far North, in part to establish communities and reinforce territoriality; nonetheless, Canadian claims of Arctic Archipelago waters as internal waters continue to be disputed by other countries.

On its extended mission, the Northern Party corrected mapping mistakes made by previous expeditions and conducted soundings of the ocean floor, enabling preliminary mapping of the continental shelf. At the end of his Arctic sojourn, Stefansson reported no great hardships during that time and claimed he and his associates could have lived for years on the ice floes. He died in 1962 at the age of 82, all the while blaming Bartlett for the *Karluk* disaster. Bartlett, in typical fashion, never publicly responded to these criticisms, although in private he expressed his definitive opinions of that "#$@&%*! liar" in his usual colourfully descriptive speech.

* * *

Nigeraurak was taken by Fred Maurer to his home in New Philadelphia, Ohio. The cat lived to a ripe old age and produced many litters of black kittens with white feet and bibs. Maurer called them all Karluk and presented some to expedition members, including Dr. Anderson and William Laird McKinlay, who responded with a gift of Scottish shortbread. He described the cat as "the only member of the expedition to survive the whole affair sleek and unscathed." Even in their most desperate moments on the ice or on the island, no one had ever considered putting Puss in the pot. Maurer joined the lecture circuit, talking about the Arctic, and got married. He then returned to Wrangel Island as part of a colonization experiment.

The infamous 1921 expedition, conceived by none other than Vilhjalmur Stefansson, who had never been there, created a diplomatic incident and resulted in four more deaths. Stefansson envisioned Wrangel as a colonized Canadian territory and the centre of a northern empire based on the riches of the surrounding polar basin. He wanted to claim it for Canada, but the Canadian government declined his request for funding because of his connection to the *Karluk* disaster. He approached the British government as well, but they were not interested. The would-be colonists were Canadian Allan Crawford; Americans Fred Maurer, Lorne Knight, and Milton Galle; and Inuit seamstress and cook Ada Blackjack, who brought along her cat, Vic, for company. They left Alaska in 1921 to lay unauthorized claim to the island for Canada and the British Empire. On September 16, 1921, the team was dropped off with assurances a ship would relieve them with another group of squatters in early 1922.

The ship sent to pick them up got stuck in the ice, and the relief trip was abandoned until the summer of 1923, when the weather improved. In the intervening time, the group quickly ran out of food and were ignorant of how to hunt game. Maurer, then twenty-nine years old, was one of the party of three desperate men who attempted to get help by recreating Bartlett's trek on foot across the ice and through the wilderness of Siberia. They left in January 1923 and were never seen again; the fourth man in the party, Lorne Knight, died of scurvy on Wrangel Island .

Ada Blackjack was now alone except for Vic, her cat. She learned to shoot game and survived on Wrangel until August 19, 1923, when a ship got in and got her out. Russia protested the attempted colonization, and Canada dropped all claims. (Even though he had been refused funding by Canada and Britain, Stefansson nevertheless planned to claim the island for Canada and the British Empire without the knowledge of anyone in authority in Ottawa. When the scheme became public in early 1922, it was at first viewed positively by Prime Minister Mackenzie King until it was pointed out that Wrangel lay outside the 141st meridian, the normally accepted end of Canada's Western Arctic boundary, and in Russian waters.)

In 1926, the Soviet Union established their sovereignty over Wrangel by forcibly relocating a small colony of Chukchi Natives from Siberia to live there permanently. In the mid-1970s, with the creation of a nature sanctuary, descendants of these original settlers were repatriated back to the mainland. The US State Department, in spite of the 1881 claiming of Wrangel Island as US territory by the crew of the *Corwin*, never asserted any territorial claim to the island.

Believing that the discovery of new land was more important than scientific research, Stefansson had often demanded access to the CAE Southern Party's resources, which, to his irritation, it resisted supplying. After the expedition, Stefansson wrote a scathing account of the Southern Party's scientists in his 1921 book, *The Friendly Arctic.* In media interviews, he made very unfriendly accusations of mutiny and insubordination against Southern Party scientists and their leader, Dr. R.M. Anderson. It was a bitter public battle that was never fully resolved.

In 1924, another Arctic expedition, this time under Captain Louis Lane on the MS *Herman* (not to be confused with the SS *Herman*, the whaling and trading ship captained by Christian Theodore Pedersen a decade earlier), made its way to nearby Herald Island, sixty kilometres east of Wrangel, where they discovered the remains of a campsite on the northwest side. A sled, a corroded rifle, ammunition, matches, hunting knives, a stove, snow goggles, a pocket compass, a silver watch, and the bones of four humans under blankets were among their findings. From the scattered debris, it looked like the small group had lived there for some time. Who were they? Could these be the *Karluk*'s four lost members Sandy Anderson, Charles Barker, John Brady, and Edmund L. Golightly, who might have missed Wrangel and ended up on Herald instead?

No definite cause of death was established, since the men appeared to have had sufficient food and the ability to hunt for more; unopened cans of pemmican and other food from the *Karluk* were discovered, along with some clothing and ammunition for the firearms. No written records or diaries were found. Lane believed the skeletons to be the members of the mate's party (because of the items found near the skeletons) and not of the scientists' party. He reported:

> The beach was strewn with driftwood and a large log lay right in the middle of the camp. On the side opposite to the sled we found the remains of the party's tents. The end had collapsed upon the bed and those in it, for as we scraped away the snow and carefully pulled the frozen canvas from what was beneath, we found parts of human skeletons. They lay as if the men had died in their sleep.

The remains and artifacts were sent to Canada for identification, but nothing more was reported until the artifacts and a human jawbone appeared for sale on eBay in 1999. They had been purchased from a Chicago museum by a couple who operated a cowboy memorabilia business in Colorado, then sold to a biographer of Bob Bartlett, Jennifer Niven, who stated: "Through some dental detective work, I was able to conclude that the jawbone belonged to First Mate Sandy Anderson."

Perhaps they had been asphyxiated by poisonous fumes of carbon monoxide from a faulty camp stove as they waited for their *Karluk* companions to arrive. The mystery of the Herald Island remains has still to be fully solved.

At the end of October 1914, John Hadley, carpenter/hunter, rejoined the Northern Party of the Canadian Arctic Expedition, becoming second officer, and later master, of the supply ship *Polar Bear*. He died of influenza in San Francisco in 1918. Hadley was the only survivor of the *Karluk* sinking and the Wrangel Island encampment to rejoin the expedition. In spite of their physical and mental trauma, some *Karluk* survivors lived long lives. Some simply vanished, such as Robert Templeman, who immigrated to Australia and was never heard from again. Second engineer Robert Williamson, who never spoke or wrote about his experience, died in Victoria in 1975 at the age of 97. Ernest Chafe wrote a short account of the experience, while John Hadley and Burt McConnell wrote descriptions of their northern adventures for Stefansson, who incorporated their material into his book *The Friendly Arctic*. Although he encouraged others to do so, Stefansson himself never went north again, restricting his activities to lecturing.

The great Norwegian explorer Roald Amundsen, who was the first to traverse the Northwest Passage in 1905 and the first to reach the South Pole in 1911, was not impressed by Stefansson. The "friendliness" of the Arctic environment, he warned, was a myth dangerous to those who "adventure into these regions, equipped only with a gun and some ammunition. If they do, death awaits them." He referred to Vilhjalmur Stefansson as "the greatest humbug alive."

William Laird McKinlayreturned to Scotland and then went off to war on the Western Front as a lieutenant with the Gordon Highlanders. He was seriously wounded and, after recuperating, returned to teaching. Back home in Scotland, McKinlay fell in love, married, and by the 1930s had risen to the position of headmaster of Mount School in Greenock, where he pioneered summer school camps. In the fall of 1917, he received a surprise visit from George Wilkins, the *Karluk*'s photographer, asking if he would be interested in joining an Antarctic expedition. It was momentarily tempting. For all the hell he had been through, there was still something tempting about the polar regions. He sometimes felt the tug of exploring different worlds but declined Wilkins's offer; he had resumed the life that suited him and would not wander far afield again.

His feet continued to give him problems throughout his life from the frostbite he had suffered, and he lost all but one of his teeth as a result of poor nutrition on Wrangel Island.

McKinlay and Bartlett shared a comradeship unique among members of the expedition. They probably discussed the circumstances around the death of George Breddy, but, although they had their suspicions, never made any definitive statements. After a debriefing in October 1914 in Ottawa, McKinlay never broached the subject again. Maybe it had been a suicide, or maybe not; who knew? The story they all told was that Breddy had died of an "accidental shooting." Even though he had given his official statement, the Supreme Court of British Columbia still requested that McKinlay make an official declaration in November 1923 before "a notary public, mayor, or chief magistrate of any city," regarding the death of George Breddy. In the declaration he made in Victoria, McKinlay stated: "The said death was caused by the accidental discharge of the deceased's revolver while he was engaged in cleaning it." Years after the expedition, McKinlay received a copy of a letter Bartlett had written to a mutual friend in November 1914:

> McKinlay is a good boy with a level head upon his shoulders, a true loyal friend, a good shipmate and a hard worker. I cannot begin to tell you of the pillar of strength he was to me and shall never be able to repay him. Strange, when we wished each other goodbye, it was as if we both grew up together and our being together just an ordinary event. I can

> truthfully say he was everything that a fellow man requires of another.

The letter meant everything to McKinlay. Until the day he died, he felt only admiration for Bartlett and what he had done.

* * *

McKinlay had kept three diaries of his 1913–14 experiences. One was scientific, for the Canadian government, and the other two were personal observations of the small joys and daily privations he and his colleagues had faced. At age 88, he published an account of the *Karluk* disaster. In 1977, he returned with his daughter to visit the islands of the Arctic Archipelago (and also Calgary, Vancouver, and Ottawa). It was an emotional visit, as memories of 1913–14 came rushing back. In another diary, he wrote:

> My writing, I must confess, had reawakened all the harrowing feelings which have bedevilled my life for so many years, but I am hoping that, once I have finished, I may find some measure of peace. After experiencing the fellowship of the army, not all the horrors of the Western Front, not the rubble of Arras, nor the hell of Ypres, nor all the mud of Flanders leading to Passchendaele, could blot out the memories of that year in the Arctic. The loyalty, the comradeship, the esprit de corps of my fellow officers and of the men it was my privilege to command, enabled us to survive the horrors of war, and I realized that this is what had been entirely

> missing up north; it was the lack of real comradeship that had left the scars, not the physical rigours and hazards of the ice pack, nor the deprivations on Wrangel Island.

Antarctic explorer Ernest Shackleton had voiced similar feelings, comparing polar hardships to war in his dedication of the account of his last expedition (1914–1917): "To my comrades who fell in the white warfare of the south and on the red fields of France and Flanders."

Reflecting on the distant past, McKinlay wrote:

> The two years, 1913 and 1914, saw the last two expeditions to the polar regions of the old historic type in the wooden ships and before the days of radio and aeroplanes—the *Karluk* to the north and Shackleton's *Endurance* to the south. Both vessels met the same fate. Both stories tell of strenuous journeys of seven or eight hundreds of miles to bring rescue. The *Endurance* story ended happily and has been fully and faithfully recorded; the other ended tragically but has never been well and truthfully documented.

McKinlay died in 1983 at the age of 95.

Although a hero to the press and the public, Captain Bob Bartlett was censured by a British Admiralty commission for taking the *Karluk* into the pack ice-infested Arctic waters and letting MacKay's group of four scientists leave the main party and head south on their own, especially since the *Karluk* was not purpose-built for exploration in the high North, and Bartlett himself had doubts about its seaworthiness. Investigations into marine disasters, and especially ones where there was loss of life, were routine. Still, on August 18, 1914, the *New York Times* reported that Captain Robert A. Bartlett had been "absolved of blame for the fate of the members of the expedition who left his party. It is too bad that Dr. Mackay, Murray, Beuchat, and Sailor Morris left the main party. But Bartlett has a paper signed by all of them, stating that they made the trip on their own initiative, and exempting him from all responsibility, and as they were not members of his crew, he had no authority to prevent them from leaving the camp."

The Royal Geographic Society granted Bartlett the Sir George Back Award for his leadership of the survivors, and he was hailed as a hero by the public and by his former *Karluk* shipmates. Many of them credited him with saving their lives, particularly William Laird McKinlay, who later wrote, "There was for me only one real hero in the whole [*Karluk*] story—Bob Bartlett. Honest, fearless, reliable, loyal, everything a man should be."

Bartlett acquired American citizenship and resumed his maritime career, commanding US transport ships during the First World War. In 1917, he again headed a rescue mission, this time as captain of the sealing schooner *Neptune*, to bring back Commander Donald MacMillan and the other members of the Crocker Land Expedition, who were stranded on the ice for four years near Etah in northwest Greenland. The expedition's mandate was to find Crocker Land, a large island supposedly seen by Robert Peary from the top of Cape Colgate in 1906. It was subsequently found to have been a fake.

Bob Bartlett never married, but in 1925, he acquired the thirty-four-metre-long schooner *Effie M. Morrissey* from an uncle. "She's all I've got," he said. "When she stops, so do I." From 1926 until his death, in addition to making many fishing and hunting trips in his beloved little *Morrissey*, Bartlett also made more than twenty voyages to the Arctic to gather specimens, aid in archaeological surveys, and correct geographical charts for patrons such as the National Geographic Society, the Smithsonian Institution, and the Museum of the American Indian, and to collect animals for zoos. The *Morrissey* was eventually retired to Mystic Seaport: The Museum of America and the Sea in the village of Mystic, near Groton, Connecticut. There is also a collection of letters at the museum from Bartlett to his close friend, Southmayd Hatch, an engineer with Socony-Vacuum Oil Company (later Mobil Oil), relating to Bartlett's travels in Greenland, Newfoundland, and the Arctic.

Although he had turned death and disaster into life-affirming victory by sheer force of will in one of Canada's little-known Arctic rescues, Bartlett received much of the financial backing for his excursions over the years from American sources, and he received far more recognition in the US than in Canada. After a life spent doing what he loved, Bartlett died of pneumonia in New York in 1946 at the age of 70, just five months after his last trip on the *Morrissey*.

What was behind Bartlett's lifelong appetite to explore one of the coldest places on Earth? He explained it this way: "The truth was I could not stop myself in pursuit of adventure. I was committed to the Arctic. I'd got the poison in my veins. When I die, I don't want a monument. I just want some boy to say I taught him how to navigate . . . and how to tell when the ice is safe."

He got the monument anyway; it was placed a short distance from his grave in Brigus, Newfoundland.

* * *

Mugpi, later known as Ruth Makpii Ipalook, was the last survivor of the ill-fated *Karluk* voyage, dying in 2008 at age 97. Throughout her life, she was known for her cheerfulness. She had survived the whole *Karluk* ordeal with only a scratch on her chin, delivered by Nigeraurak, who did not appreciate the child's teasing. She left the *Bear* in Nome, along with her parents, Kuraluk and Kiruk, and her sister Helen for the long overland trip back home to Point Barrow. Mugpi and Helen were eventually joined by two brothers, one of whom their parents named Bartlett. Mugpi married Fred Ipalook, and they had nine children.

The first Canadian Arctic Expedition began with the loss of eleven men and its flagship. In total, some 150 people spent varying amounts of time assigned to expedition work over its extended lifespan. The initial government budget for the entire expedition had been $75,000, a figure

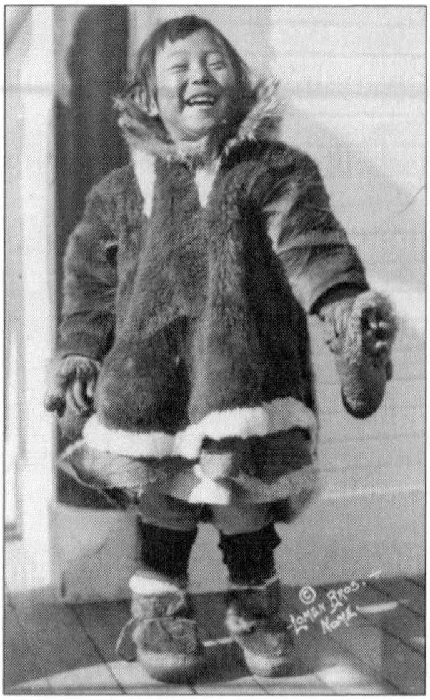

(left) Nigeraurak, the ship's cat, taking the sun at Icy Spit, Wrangel Island, May 1914. LIBRARY AND ARCHIVES CANADA C-071039
(right) Mugpi, from Point Barrow, Alaska, the youngest member of the *Karluk* party. LIBRARY AND ARCHIVES CANADA PA-105139

that mushroomed to $559,972 by its end in 1918. The only *Karluk* memorabilia known to exist are a few artifacts at the Maritime Museum in Victoria, British Columbia, from the time of her refurbishment in Esquimalt: a carved, walrus-ivory tusk model of the ship made by a crew member, a paddle marked *Karluk*, and some objects recovered by Captain Louis Lane from Herald Island in 1924. A brass deck plate from the ship was stolen from the museum in the 1970s.

Epilogue

ALTHOUGH OVERSHADOWED IN THE PUBLIC mind by the events of the First World War, the first Canadian Arctic Expedition staked Canada's claim to thousands of square kilometres of its northern boundaries and the Arctic Archipelago. It was one of the greatest scientific feats and epic journeys of the early twentieth century. The expedition discovered, mapped, and named islands of the Arctic previously unknown to non-Natives, including Brock, Mackenzie King, Borden, Meighen, and Lougheed Islands. Its experts collected important scientific and cultural knowledge through observations, 4,000 photographs, 2,743 metres of film (with a running time of an hour), specimens of animals, plants, rocks, and fossils, as well as artifacts of the Copper Inuit and Inuvialuit cultures that defined polar life of the period in the Western Arctic.

Through trade, the expedition had a significant impact on Indigenous lifestyles by establishing permanent settlements, a wage economy, and new technologies such as needles, matches, rifles, and ammunition in exchange for clothes, bows, arrows, stone lamps, and pots. Such transactions had positive and negative effects on the Inuit.

The fourteen volumes published by the CAE include scientific reports on topics such as mammals, birds, insects, fishes, crustaceans, molluscs, plankton, tides, geography, geology, botany, and archaeology, as well as Inuit folklore, songs, language, and technology. Collected specimens and reports are now housed in the Canadian Museum of History, the Canadian Museum of Nature, and Library and Archives Canada, all located in or near Ottawa.

In 1926, the Canadian government, at the insistence of Belle Anderson, wife of Dr. Rudolph Anderson, leader of the CAE Southern Party, dedicated an official memorial plaque listing all sixteen members of the Northern Party (including the five *Karluk* scientists) and the Southern Party who died "for Canada and for science" during the entire expedition. (At least the CAE had survivors, unlike the doomed but better-known British expedition of Sir John Franklin to find the Northwest Passage in 1845.)

Belle Anderson understood the contentious nature of the relationship between Vilhjalmur Stefansson, CAE head and leader of the Northern Party, and the CAE scientists. She lobbied relentlessly for public recognition of the dead scientists' services because their colleagues, who still had positions in the civil service, were prevented from doing so by politics and the terms and conditions of their continued employment. Bearing the inscription, "In Memory of Those Who Perished—Canadian Arctic Expedition 1913–18," a commorative plaque was hung in the entrance to the Public Archives of Canada in Ottawa but disappeared in the 1960s, when the building was demolished and offices were moved to another location. It had disappeared, just like the *Karluk*.

Other memorials still stand. In 1978, Hawthorne Cottage, Captain Bob Bartlett's family home in Brigus, Newfoundland, was designated a National Historic Site of Canada and classified a Federal Heritage Building in 1993 by Parks Canada. Constructed in 1830 by a local merchant, it is considered a rare example of the *orné* (decorated) style of the "picturesque" (rustic) architectural movement of the late eighteenth and early nineteenth centuries. Bartlett himself had been designated a Person of National Historic Significance in 1969 for "his role in Arctic exploration."

By the early twenty-first century, federal agencies were commemorating both the heroic captain and the passage of time. In 2009, Canada Post Corporation released a stamp honouring Captain Bartlett, who was pictured holding a sextant, an instrument used to measure latitude and longitude at sea, against an icy blue-and-white background.

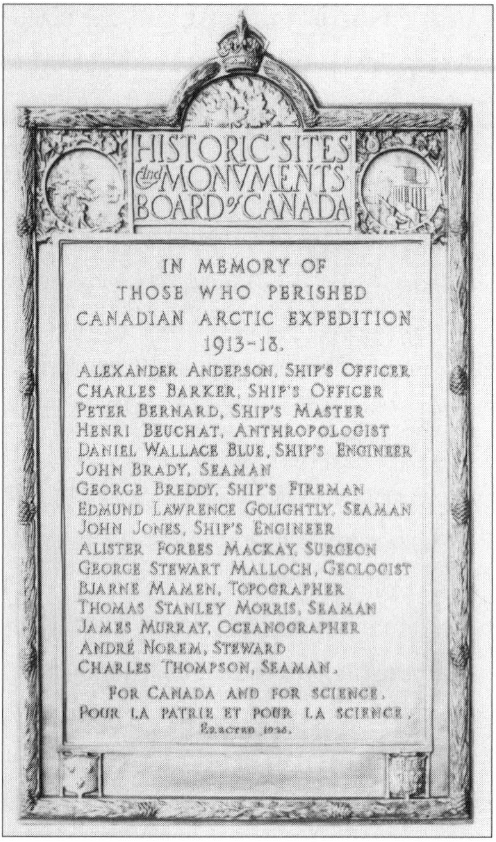

This memorial to the deceased members of the CAE hung for several years in the Public Archives in Ottawa but went missing in the 1960s. RUDOLPH MARTIN ANDERSON/LIBRARY AND ARCHIVES CANADA C-02596

Epilogue

In 2013, the Royal Canadian Mint unveiled two twenty-five-cent memorial circulation coins, one to celebrate the "100th Anniversary of the Canadian Arctic Expedition" and the other one representing "Life in the North."

Lying astride the 180th meridian of longitude, Wrangel Island is in both the western and eastern hemispheres. Wrangel and Herald Islands are the only land habitats for wildlife in the Chukchi Sea. In 1976, after pressure from Russian scientists, Wrangel's landscape of low-lying lichens and gneisses—plus its surrounding waters, which are rarely free of pack ice—were classified as a *zapovednik*, a nature reserve.

With no significant oil reserves, the area has mercifully been left alone to function as a natural laboratory for scientific study of Pacific walrus, polar bears, and grey whales. Wrangel is now one of the world's most protected nature preserves, accessible only by icebreaker in summer or helicopter in winter, and only if you are granted a rare visitor permit. An Arctic tundra biosphere, it is administered by the Russian government. The wind howls almost constantly, and winters are long and dark, with no sun from November to January. Snow covers everything 240 days a year, but spring brings a short burst of life. Flowers colour the tundra between swollen rivers, and birds return to nest. Wrangel is the northernmost nesting ground for a hundred migratory bird species (many endangered) and the only snow-goose nesting colony in Asia.

Walruses rest on sandspits to give birth, and female bears come out of their dens with cubs. Wrangel is also home to snowy owls, muskoxen, Arctic foxes, reindeer, and lemmings—but the island has no mosquitoes, unlike the Siberian mainland.

Some 417 species and subspecies of plants have been identified, double that of any other Arctic territory of comparable size.

In 2004, the unique ecosystem of both Wrangel and Herald Islands, with their surrounding waters, was added to the UNESCO World Heritage List.

* * *

List of survivors and non-survivors of the *Karluk* voyage:

Crew members

Name	**Occupation**	**Age**	**Fate**
Robert Abram Bartlett	Captain	36	Survived
Alexander "Sandy" Anderson	First Officer	27	Died
Charles Barker	Second Officer	20s	Died
John Munro	Chief Engineer	30s	Survived
Robert Williamson	Second Engineer	36	Survived
John Brady	Seaman	20s	Died
Edmund Lawrence Golightly	Seaman	20s	Died
T. Stanley Morris	Seaman	26	Died
Hugh "Clam" Williams	Seaman	20s	Survived
George Breddy	Fireman	20s	Killed (?)
Fred Maurer	Fireman	21	Survived
John Hadley	Carpenter	57	Survived
Robert "Bob" Templeman	Cook/Steward	29	Survived
Ernest "Charlie" Chafe	Mess Steward	19	Survived

Scientific members

Name	**Occupation**	**Age**	**Fate**
Vilhjalmur Stefansson	Leader	33	Left ship
Henri Beuchat	Anthropologist	34	Died

Epilogue

Diamond Jenness	Anthropologist	27	Left ship
Alistair Forbes-Mackay	Medical Officer	35	Died
George Stewart Malloch	Geologist	33	Died
Bjarne Mamen	Topographer/ Forester	22	Died
Burt McConnell	Secretary	24	Left ship
William Laird McKinlay	Magnetician/ Meteorologist	24	Survived
James Murray	Oceanographer	46	Died
George H. Wilkins	Photographer	24	Left ship

Inuit members

Name	Occupation	Age	Fate
Pauyuraq "Jerry"	Hunter	20s	Left ship
Asecaq "Jimmy"	Hunter	20s	Left ship
Kataktovik "Claude"	Hunter	19	Survived
Kuraluk	Hunter	20s	Survived
Kiruk "Auntie"	Seamstress/Cook	20s	Survived
Qagguluk "Helen"	Child	8	Survived
Mugpi "Ruth"	Child	3	Survived

Animal members

Name	Occupation	Age	Fate
Nigeraurak	Ship's cat	Kitten	Survived
Huskies (thirty)	Sled dogs	Unknown	Unknown

Selected Bibliography

Balkan, Evan L. *Shipwrecked! Deadly Adventures and Disasters at Sea*, Birmingham, AL: Menasha Ridge Press, 2008.

Bartlett, Captain Robert A., with Ralph T. Hale. *The Last Voyage of the Karluk: Shipwreck and Rescue in the Arctic*. St. John's, NL: Flanker Press Ltd., 2007.

Horwood, Howard. *Bartlett: The Great Explorer*. Toronto: Doubleday Canada, 1977.

Jenness, Stuart E. *Stefansson, Dr. Anderson and the Canadian Arctic Expedition, 1913–1918: A Story of Exploration, Science and Sovereignty*. Gatineau, QC: Canadian Museum of Civilization Corporation, 2011.

Leslie, Edward E. *Desperate Journeys, Abandoned Souls: True Stories of Castaways and Other Survivors*. Boston: HMH Mariner Books, 1998.

McKinlay, William Laird. Karluk*: The Great Untold Story of Arctic Exploration*. London: Weidenfeld and Nicolson Limited, 1976.

Niven, Jennifer. *The Ice Master: The Doomed 1913 Voyage of the* Karluk. New York: Hyperion Books, 2000.

Stefansson, Vilhjalmur. *The Friendly Arctic: The Story of Five Years in Polar Regions*. New York: The Macmillan Company, 1921.

Walters, Eric. *Trapped in Ice*. Toronto: Puffin Canada, Penguin Group, 1997.

Index

Index

About the Author

L.D. Cross is the author of numerous business and lifestyle articles that have appeared in Canadian and US publications. She has written many books in the Amazing Stories series dealing with unique aspects of Canadian history, including *Ottawa Titans: Fortune and Fame in the Early Days of Canada's Capital*; *Spies in Our Midst: The Incredible Story of Igor Gouzenko, Cold War Spy*; *The Quest for the Northwest Passage: Exploring the Elusive Route Through Canada's Arctic Waters*; *The Underground Railroad: The Long Journey to Freedom in Canada*; *Treasure Under the Tundra: Canada's Arctic Diamonds*; *Code Name Habbakuk: A Secret Ship Made of Ice*; *Flying on Instinct: Canada's Bush Pilot Pioneers*; and *Rocky Mountain Marvels: High Peaks Engineering.* She is also co-author, with physician Marilyn Daryawish, of *Marriage is a Business* and *Inside Outside: In Conversation with a Doctor and a Clothing Designer.*

Cross's creative non-fiction has been recognized by the International Association of Business Communicators' EXCEL Awards for features and editorial writing, as well as the National Mature Media Awards for her articles about seniors. In 2011, her book *The Underground Railroad: The Long Journey to Freedom in Canada* received the inaugural Ontario Historical Society Huguenot Award honouring "the best book in Ontario published in the past three years which has brought public awareness to the principles of freedom of consciousness and freedom of thought."